understanding **virtue ethics**

Understanding Movements in Modern Thought
Series Editor: Jack Reynolds

This series provides short, accessible and lively introductions to the major schools, movements and traditions in philosophy and the history of ideas since the beginning of the Enlightenment. All books in the series are written for undergraduates meeting the subject for the first time.

Published

Understanding Existentialism
Jack Reynolds

Understanding Poststructuralism
James Williams

Understanding Virtue Ethics
Stan van Hooft

Forthcoming titles include

Understanding Empiricism
Robert Meyers

Understanding Ethics
Tim Chappell

Understanding Feminism
Peta Bowden and Jane Mummery

Understanding German Idealism
Will Dudley

Understanding Hegelianism
Robert Sinnerbrink

Understanding Hermeneutics
Lawrence Schmidt

Understanding Naturalism
Jack Ritchie

Understanding Phenomenology
David Cerbone

Understanding Rationalism
Charlie Heunemann

Understanding Utilitarianism
Tim Mulgan

understanding **virtue ethics**

Stan van Hooft

First published in 2006 by Acumen

Acumen Publishing Limited
15a Lewins Yard
East Street
Chesham
Bucks HP5 1HQ
www.acumenpublishing.co.uk

ISBN 1-84465-044-8   (hardcover)
ISBN 1-84465-045-6   (paperback)

British Library Cataloguing-in-Publication Data
A catalogue record for this book is available from the British Library.

Designed and typeset by Kate Williams, Swansea.
Printed and bound in Malta by Gutenberg Press.

Contents

Introduction

Virtue

The word "virtue" derives from the Latin *virtus* meaning "excellence", "capacity" or "ability". In this sense, to have virtue is to have the power or ability to achieve something. More commonly in modern English the word has come to refer to a disposition or a pattern in someone's character or personality that leads them to act morally. It refers to traits of character that we find admirable. Examples of virtue include generosity, honesty, courage, patience, good humour and friendliness.

Different societies emphasize different virtues. Our society expresses admiration for the traits of character that lead to success in entrepreneurial activities. We count as a virtue the willingness to take risks and to compete vigorously with others in business. We praise these traits in sport as well. In other contexts, and more often among women, we praise such virtues as caring and nurturance. Some religions emphasize humility and meekness, whereas if you were in the army you would be urged to display courage and assertiveness as well as obedience (if that is not contradictory). Moreover, what people take to be virtuous changes over time. The virtues we look for in our young people today differ from those that were sought in previous ages (to be "seen but not heard", for example).

But these points seem to lead to some strange conclusions. They suggest that virtues are relative to social and cultural contexts. Among themselves, bank robbers probably admire bravado displayed during bank robberies and so it would seem that, although the activity is immoral, we would have to accept that bank robbers could describe each other as having the virtue of bravado. It might seem that virtue terms are relative to the social groups in which they are used rather than to absolute moral standards. These sorts of problems take us from our everyday intuitions about what is right and wrong and what is virtuous or not, towards a rational scrutiny of those intuitions. That is to say, they introduce us to moral theory.

The purposes of moral theory

Morality tells us what we ought to do in a specific range of circumstances, whereas moral theory (sometimes called "ethics") is the study of morality. The purposes of moral theory are various. Perhaps the most general task moral theorists set themselves is to understand what morality is. Is it a set of dispositions engrained in our genes in the way that the social habits of chimpanzees are? Is it a set of conventions we have created throughout history in order to structure our social lives? How do the rules of morality differ from religious rules such as the Jewish injunction to eat only kosher food? What is morality for? What does it seek to achieve? Does it serve an individual's concern about personal salvation, happiness or staying out of jail, or does it have a communal purpose such as the creation of peace and social progress? What distinguishes and unifies morality? Is it a set of commands from God or a set of norms that derive from a single overarching principle? Is there a single goal that human beings pursue in the light of which some traits of character and not others will be virtuous? Moral theorists bring a variety of answers to these questions.

A second purpose of moral theory is to establish what we are obliged to do, what we are forbidden from doing, what we are permitted to do and what it would be good for us to do even when it is not obligatory. In this sense, moral theory is *prescriptive*. It prescribes to us what our duties are or what it would be virtuous to do. A paradigm example of such prescriptions will be the Ten Commandments of the Judaeo-Christian tradition, which include such prescriptions as "Thou shalt not kill" and "Thou shalt not covet thy neighbour's goods". The first of these prohibits a kind of action, while the second prohibits an attitude or desire. Given that such prescriptions, along with prohibitions against lying and cheating, are well known and hardly contentious, it may be wondered whether contemporary moral theorists would have much to add to such traditional norms. No one today seriously doubts that the norms that forbid lying, cheating and murder are valid. But even that large range of moral norms that everyone accepts, at least in general terms, and that are not therefore the subject of much debate needs to be applied. We all know that it is wrong to lie, cheat or kill people unless there are very acute extenuating circumstances. But just what these circumstances might be will be an object of debate among ethicists. Debate over issues such as euthanasia and abortion are examples where moral theorists debate how to apply the rule against killing human beings so as to prescribe that one course of action is wrong while another is right.

A third question that many moral theorists ask will be just why our moral norms are valid. Here their purpose will not be to convince us of new norms, of the need to revise old ones or of the requirement to apply them consistently, but rather to understand why those prescriptions are normative at all. Why are duties obligatory as opposed to merely advisory? It might be prudent to avoid such actions, but just why is it *wrong* to lie, to cheat or to commit murder? Here the task of moral theory will be not so much to prescribe as to *justify* our norms. The Ten Commandments can offer us an example once again. For religious believers, these norms are obligatory because God has commanded them. God's command explains or justifies why we are obliged to obey them. In the natural law tradition it is argued that God has made human beings with a human nature that incorporates a certain set of goals and tendencies and that our moral obligations are binding upon us because they fulfil these goals and tendencies. For secular thinkers, it is often argued that moral norms are obligatory because they are based on reason. The simplest of these views suggests that moral rules are obligatory because they lead to the greatest happiness for the greatest number of affected beings, while the most sophisticated suggests that the power of reason itself makes our norms obligatory given that we are free and rational beings. Whatever metaphysical views philosophers subscribe to as a background to their moral thinking (whether they believe in God or in human freedom, for example), what they are seeking to do when they offer such explanations is to justify moral norms by showing what they are based on and what reasons can be adduced to support them.

A fourth task of moral theory is to *describe* our moral lives to us. This task has sometimes been called "moral psychology". It is the task of making clear how people experience being under an obligation, actually make moral decisions, think about moral issues or think about themselves as moral agents. Although it sounds as if this would be an empirical study, moral theorists seldom make use of data from such social sciences as psychology, anthropology and sociology. Rather, they draw upon philosophical theories about what it is to be a human being: theories such as those that suggest we possess a rational soul, or a free will, or a mind that is furnished with natural sentiments and inclinations. One reason why such studies are important is that it would be useless to prescribe norms that are too stringent for fallible and finite human beings to follow. For example, it might be argued that we cannot have a moral obligation to help every needy person in the world because it is beyond our capacity to do so. And such an incapacity might not be based just on our not having the resources to help everyone, but also on the limited range of our psychological abilities to care about others. In this and other ways claims about our moral psychology are relevant to what norms it is realistic to prescribe for human beings. Moreover, the justification of our moral norms must be sensitive to what we are as human beings. For example, if we are more influenced by our emotions than we are by our reason, then it might be best not to posit pure reason as the basis of our norms.

As differing strands within moral theory, the ethics of duty and virtue ethics share these four tasks:

- to understand morality;
- to prescribe norms;
- to justify those norms; and
- to describe how they fit into our lives.

But they differ in the way that they fulfil these tasks and also in the emphasis that they place upon them.

Structure of the book

Virtue ethics has emerged in the past few decades as an important strand within moral theory. Accordingly it must fulfil the four tasks of moral theory listed above. It is my contention that virtue ethics meets this challenge as well as, if not better than, the ethics of duty. However, this short book cannot undertake to justify this bold assertion. It must have the more modest goal of explicating what virtue ethics is and how it addresses the four tasks that I have described.

Chapter 1 will detail a number of distinctions between virtue ethics and the ethics of duty. This chapter encapsulates a great deal of the recent discussion of virtue ethics that was inaugurated by such writers as Elizabeth Anscombe, Philippa Foot, Alasdair MacIntyre, Michael

Stocker and Bernard Williams and carried on by such authors as Rosalind Hursthouse, Christine Swanton and Michael Slote. It is in this chapter that I suggest that virtue ethics is superior to an ethics of duty, although it is not until the next few chapters that I can argue for this claim. Although not all virtue ethicists are inspired by Aristotle, he is important to the thinking of most of them. Accordingly, Chapter 2 details Aristotle's theory. In Chapter 3 I show how David Hume contributed a new focus on the emotions to moral psychology and virtue ethics, I discuss Nietzsche in order to explain the existential importance that virtue gained with his emphasis on self-affirmation, and then show how this stress on self-affirmation makes it difficult to theorize concern for others. I go on to explain how Emmanuel Levinas's theory of ethics entails that such self-affirmation cannot take place without concern for other people. The notion of virtue requires a description of human existence in which our responsibility for others can be seen to be more than a morally required addition to our lives. It is the very basis of our identity. I appeal to the thought of Paul Ricoeur in Chapter 4 in order to show how virtue ethics can take account of the demands of justice and of morality objectively conceived. This is a task that critics of virtue ethics have alleged is beyond its capacity because it seems to depend on contingent virtuous motivations in the agent.

If Chapters 2–4 provide the theoretical bases for an ethics of duty, the following chapters provide some applications. There is little point in a book on ethics if it does not show how it might be applied. In Chapter 5 I describe some virtues that I consider important in our day, and in Chapter 6 I illustrate how virtue ethics can be relevant to problems in applied ethics. This last is another task that critics have alleged is difficult on the grounds that the moral principles that people must follow need to be established objectively. This contrast between the alleged objectivity of the norms postulated by the ethics of duty and the subjective motivational basis of virtue ethics is just one of the many contrasts between the two traditions that we shall need to explore in the chapters that follow.

one

Distinguishing virtue ethics from the ethics of duty

Most philosophical discussions of ethics and morality in the past several hundred years have focused on duty. As a result, the current renewal of interest in virtue ethics has been articulated by way of drawing contrasts between the ethics of duty and virtue ethics. Indeed, much of the contemporary understanding of virtue ethics has been developed by criticizing the ethics of duty. I shall follow this pattern by building my discussion in this chapter around the table of distinctions in Table 1. (And I shall explicate the technical terms in Table 1 in the text that follows.)

As I elucidate Table 1 it needs to be remembered that I am not in a position to fully explicate the points in the column headed "The ethics of duty". This phrase covers a number of different moral theories and each of them has been widely discussed and elaborated in a variety of ways. I cannot hope to do justice to all the complexities and nuances that moral theorists have developed over hundreds of years. I shall need to assume that the reader has a sufficiently broad familiarity with these traditions to allow me not to explicate them more fully. Moreover, there are many proponents of the ethics of duty who argue that the criticisms that virtue ethicists have made can be answered and that the characterizations of duty ethics that I list below do not apply to their particular enunciations of that tradition. They could well accuse me of offering a caricature of their position. It would be beyond the scope of this book to detail all of these discussions. Another book in this series, *Understanding Ethical Theory*, would be a good place to begin to explore these many issues. As for the column headed "Virtue ethics", what I say in this chapter will be of a preliminary nature and much of it will be explained further, and

Table 1 Some distinctions between the ethics of duty and virtue ethics

Theme		The ethics of duty	Virtue ethics
What morality is about	I	Defines the moral sphere	Extends beyond the moral sphere
	II	Assumes the centrality of altruism	Accepts that the self is ethically important
	III	Asks "What should I do?"	Asks "What should I be?" or "How should I live?"
Moral terminology	I	Deontic	Aretaic
	II	Focus on action	Focus on character
	III	"Thin" concepts	"Thick" concepts
	IV	Goodness defined in terms of rightness	Goodness defined as human excellence
The nature of norms	I	"Practical necessity" seen as obligation and obedience	"Practical necessity" seen as expression of character and response to values
	II	Absolute, leading to moral dilemmas	Varying in stringency, requiring judgement
	III	Based on general principles	Responsive to particular considerations
	IV	Justified by reason	Influenced by emotion
	V	Justice perspective	Caring perspective
	VI	Impartial	Partial
	VII	Reasons externalism	Reasons internalism
	VIII	Moral realism	Social construction of ethics
The basis of norms	I	Based on metaphysics or *a priori* reason	Intuitions grounded in community traditions
	II	Foundationalism	Hermeneutics
	III	Universal	Culture-relative
Moral psychology	I	Dualism: goodness inheres in the will or the soul	Holism: virtue inheres in the whole person
	II	Assumes the lucidity of consciousness to ground voluntariness.	Accepts the opacity of consciousness. Decisions are often obscure to the agent.
	III	Persons are "social atoms"	Human beings are interdependent and social
The nature of moral judgements about others	I	Agent-neutral	Agent-relative
	II	Supererogatory actions are difficult to understand	Supererogatory actions seen as virtuous

argued for, in the chapters that follow. In this sense, the present exposition sets the agenda for the rest of the book.

What morality is about

I

Whereas duty ethics defines the scope of morality, virtue ethics extends beyond the sphere of the moral. Morality urges us to avoid such wrongful activities as cheating, lying, theft, adultery and murder. More positively, moral injunctions deal with such issues as respecting others (rather than exploiting them by cheating or misleading them), respecting property rights, honouring sexual relations and acknowledging the sanctity of life. These are the core issues with which morality universally concerns itself. The principles on these matters that reasonable people place before themselves or inherit from their moral and religious traditions will be definitive of what morality is. Although it may not always be easy to distinguish a moral issue from a non-moral one, the core concepts of morality will be clear enough and will be covered by norms with which most people will be familiar. They are mostly concerned with how we relate to other people and to their property, life and liberties. These moral issues define the range of concerns of an ethics of duty.

In contrast, the discourse of virtue ethics ranges much more widely than this relatively delimited moral sphere. Using the language of virtue ethics, a person might be praised for being honest, courageous, generous, punctual, amiable or courteous. But the last three of these are not moral qualities in themselves. They are certainly qualities that we admire in people, they may even be useful qualities, but we do not usually condemn someone as immoral who does not display them. Unless there is great harm caused by it, we do not usually think of someone's being late for an appointment as a *moral* failure. In this way, virtue ethics extends beyond the sphere of the moral – the sphere of those other-regarding actions that are either obligatory, forbidden or morally permitted – to include admirable qualities that do not have specifically moral significance and that are not commanded by the moral law.

II

Much of duty ethics focuses on our obligations towards others. The assumption that most duty ethicists make is that the point of morality is to order our relationships with others and with society. They would argue that morality has to do with our obligations to other people rather than with our concern for ourselves or our own interests. For such theorists the latter concerns come under the heading of "prudence", whereas morality is the normative structure that we give to our altruism. It is wrong to lie, steal and murder because of the harms that this does to others, and it is obligatory to help others and to adhere to the norms of justice because of the benefit that this will bring to others. Although some moral theorists do speak of duties that we have to ourselves – for example, the duty to develop our talents – this is seen by many theorists to be a problematic category of duties unless they can be shown to have value for people other than the individual in question.

In contrast, virtue ethics embraces the self of the agent among its concerns. A virtue ethicist does not need to explain why it is virtuous to develop our talents by showing that doing so would be of benefit to others, for example. We admire people who strive for excellence for its own sake whether or not their doing so benefits others. The achievements of great artists and sports heroes are admired and described with such virtue terms as "perseverance", "tenacity" and "courage" even though they are not of direct moral significance by being of readily identifiable benefit to other people. Indeed, it has been suggested that the point of being virtuous is not so much that it helps us fulfil our moral obligations towards others – although they may indeed have this benefit – but to ensure that we ourselves flourish in a variety of ways. To flourish in this context means more than just to succeed in our projects and to fulfil our aspirations. It also means to live up to the standards of excellence that we set ourselves and that our communities or societies hold out to us. It is to be at peace with ourselves and to be in harmony with our communities. It is to be integrated in the sense of avoiding inner conflict between our feelings, desires and ways of being. It is to have a grasp on what our lives are about and what is important to us and to those for whom we care. I shall elaborate on these ideals of human excellence in later chapters. For the moment the point to note is that the flourishing of the self is among the goals of virtue ethics in a way that the ethics of duty, with its focus upon others, would find uncomfortable. Accordingly, for a virtue ethicist, it will be among the goals of moral theory to describe what human flourishing consists in and how the virtues help us achieve it.

III

The central question for an ethics of duty is: what should I do? When a moral agent, as conceived by an ethics of duty, finds himself in a morally complex situation he will ask himself what it is his duty to do. He will consider what moral norms or principles apply to the situation and seek to apply them. Virtue ethics, in contrast, will consider what sort of person the agent should be and what sort of life they should lead. Although this question is still "practical" in the sense that it addresses what the agent is to do in a given situation, it will not answer this question primarily by consulting principles, norms or policies that apply to such situations in general. Rather, it will seek to answer it by considering the agent's own character along with other morally salient features of the situation. Virtuous agents will seek to express who they are and to develop themselves as who they are in what they do. If it is a matter of telling the truth when it is difficult to do so, the agent will not consider the action objectively under the general principle that anyone in any situation should tell the truth, but will rather consider what an honest person would do, and she will be motivated to do that to the extent that she wants to be an honest person.

I need to put this point carefully. I would not want to suggest that an honest person tells the truth for the sake of being an honest person. This would be an inappropriately self-centred motivation. We do not act virtuously for the sake of being virtuous. Rather, an honest person tells the truth because she loves the truth. She acknowledges the value of truth. She tells the truth for the sake of the truth. It is her love of the truth – or her respect for the truth if "love" is too emotional a term – that moves her to do the more difficult and virtuous thing, rather than her desire to be honest. She does express her desire to be honest in telling the truth and she does develop herself as an honest person in doing so, but her reason or motivation for doing so is that she considers that the truth is important in itself. So the distinction that some virtue ethicists make between the ethics of duty and virtue ethics by saying that the former asks "What should I do?" and the latter asks "What should I be?" can be somewhat misleading. In a difficult practical situation one is always led to ask what one should do. It is just that the virtuous person expresses who they are when they act and, in acting, they develop who they are. An honest person expresses and develops herself as honest when she acts for the sake of the truth. One might imagine that a person who is not fully formed in virtue and who is trying to become virtuous might decide to tell the truth so that they will become honest, but a relatively mature virtuous person simply loves the truth and acts for the sake of it.

> Moral action, in the full-blooded sense of action from moral virtue, need not be rule following conduct or performed under the conception of the virtue in question or indeed under any explicitly moral concept, such as that of (moral) duty.   Robert Audi, *Moral Knowledge and Ethical Character*, 292

Moral terminology

I

An ethics of duty uses "deontic" terms (from the ancient Greek term meaning "necessity") such as "right", "wrong", "obligatory" or "forbidden". These terms refer to what it is "necessary" to do, what we "must" do, or what we "have to" do. They describe our obligations and duties. Moreover, they are used to render a summary judgement, all things considered, on the moral status of an action or a type of action. Accordingly, the ethics of duty is most concerned with the rightness or wrongness of actions, both in the individual case where it asks whether an action that an agent is considering performing or has performed in the past is right or wrong, and in the case of general norms where it asks whether such actions as procuring abortions or such practices as the factory farming of animals are right or wrong. In contrast, virtue ethics uses "aretaic" terms (from the Greek term meaning "virtue" or "excellence") such as "virtuous", "good", "admirable" and, more specifically, "honest", "courageous" or "modest". These terms also render a judgement on actions but, as well, they make reference to the internal state of the agent.

II

Duty ethics is pre-eminently concerned with action whereas virtue ethics focuses somewhat more on the agent. Although it does use aretaic terms to describe actions, virtue ethics is more interested in the moral condition of the agent than in whether her action is right or wrong. It focuses on the agent's character and on the virtues that make up that character. The agent's actions are seen as expressions of that character and are therefore not the primary object of attention. Even when a virtue ethicist says that a particular action was courageous, for example, this judgement is primarily about the agent's state of virtue. Such a judgement does not just say that the action appeared to be courageous, but that the agent was courageous in performing it. Accordingly, the notion of "character" is central to virtue ethics.

This raises the question of what we mean by the term "character". Compare the psychologist's term "personality" or the way in which dog-breeders talk of the friendly "nature" that some breeds have. These terms sum up the behaviour of the persons or dogs being referred to. There is nothing to observe other than that behaviour. If the behaviour falls into a consistent pattern it is described as evincing a certain sort of character, personality or nature: a person who smiles a lot and gets on easily with people is said to have an outgoing personality; a dog that is good with small children is said to have a sweet nature; and a person who consistently tells the truth is described as being of honest character. What is being described here would seem to be the behaviour.

However, there does seem to be more here than just a summary description of behaviour taken by itself. As is clear from the dog-breeding case, personalities can be shaped by causes and can have causal effects on behaviour. That a sweet nature can be bred shows that it is genetic. Although we may only know what such a nature is from seeing the behaviour it gives rise to, it does seem to be something definite in the genetic makeup of the dog: something that has behavioural effects. Perhaps what psychologists refer to as "personality" is also like this. Although there will be some aspects of it that are acquired through experience, there may also be a genetic element. You may be naturally disposed to being cheerful, and if you have many positive experiences during your life this will reinforce your cheery personality, whereas if you have many disappointments you might lose that natural disposition. So there does seem to be something real within you, whether it is genetic or the result of experience, which comes to expression in your behaviour. It may not be possible to identify it apart from the behaviour that expresses it, but it will be something that structures your behavioural repertoire and provides a motivational basis for your actions. I would suggest that the concept of "character" operates in much the same way. Although it is not an entity or aspect of us that we can identify in its own right, it makes sense to think of it as more than just a summary of what we characteristically do. It is created by our upbringing and by our own efforts at self-formation, perhaps on the basis of natural predispositions that we acquire genetically, and it comes to expression in much of what we do. It takes a greater effort to act in a way that is contrary to our character than to act in a way that is consistent with it. And this shows that it is something real with causal influences on our lives. Perhaps we should consider it to be somewhat like a skill at playing a musical instrument: a genetically enabled disposition that we acquire by habit or training and by a commitment to its values.

> It would be a great improvement if, instead of "morally wrong", one always named a genus such as "untruthful", "unchaste", "unjust". We should no longer ask whether doing something was "wrong", passing directly from some description of an action to this notion; we should ask whether, e.g., it was unjust; and the answer would sometimes be clear at once.
>
> G. E. M. Anscombe, "Modern Moral Philosophy", 10

III

Duty ethics is said to make use of "thin" concepts, whereas virtue ethics uses "thick" concepts. This is an implication of saying that duty ethics uses deontic terms and is primarily concerned with whether an action is right or wrong. These are "thin" concepts because they do not offer us much in the way of a description of the action. We do not learn anything about an action when we describe it as "wrong" except that it is morally forbidden. To say of murder that it is wrong is to give no clue as to what it is about an act of murder that makes it wrong or what it is about the agent that attracts our moral condemnation. Indeed, it might even be a tautology that tells us nothing. After all a "murder" is defined as a wrongful killing of a human being. So to say that murder is wrong is to say something that is true by definition. It gives us no substantive information at all. To describe an action as "courageous" or "generous", on the other hand, is to convey considerably more information. In the first case it suggests that the situation in which the action was performed was one of danger to the agent. It suggests that the agent acted with fortitude and commitment in the face of that danger. It suggests that such fortitude and commitment are excellent ways of being a human being. In this way, because a lot of meaning is conveyed in it, the word "courageous" is deemed to be a "thick" concept. Virtue terms are generally thick in this way.

IV

For the ethics of duty, moral goodness is defined in relation to what is demanded by the moral law or by moral principles and rules. For human beings to be good is simply for them to act rightly for the right reasons. But this is a thin conception of goodness. It defines goodness as little more than avoiding wrongdoing. What virtue ethics places before us, on the other hand, are ideals of goodness for human beings. It does not ask what would be morally right so much as what would constitute human excellence. Very often, virtue ethics begins by articulating a theory about human beings and then builds ideals of human excellence on that basis. If the purpose of a knife is to cut things, then an excellent knife is one that cuts things well. In this way, by understanding what a knife is and what it is for, we can define what a good knife would be. In the same way, if we can say what a human being is in terms of its function, we will be able to say what it is to be an excellent or good human being.

Although philosophers have spent an enormous amount of time on the question, it is not difficult to develop an intuitively acceptable theory of what human beings are. Taking adult, fully competent human beings as a paradigm case, we could suggest that among the central and distinctive features of such human beings is that they are rational, social, creative and communicative. We are rational in that we think about what we might do, plan for our futures and seek to establish satisfactory arrangements for living a successful human life. We are social in that we live in families, communities and societies and could hardly survive without these social arrangements. We are creative in that we find new solutions to practical problems, develop the arts and continually seek to improve the ways we do things. And we are communicative in that we use language not just to increase the efficiency of practical projects, but also to express our ideas and feelings, develop our cultures and generally lubricate our social lives. I am not saying that these are the only important qualities of human beings. But they will do in order for me to illustrate my point. Nor am I suggesting that we are entirely unique in evincing these qualities. Many animals may be rational, social, creative and communicative in rudimentary ways as well. The argument does not depend on these qualities being unique to human beings. The argument says that if these are qualities that mark human existence, then a good human being is one who displays these qualities to an excellent degree. For human beings goodness does not consist just in obeying the moral law or adhering to moral principles. It consists in doing well what is in us as human beings to do. A good individual is one who is good as a human being. Accordingly, a fully developed theory of virtue ethics will include a fully developed account of what it is to be a human being and will then suggest that being virtuous consists in being a human being excellently.

The nature of norms

I

The nature of moral and other norms differs in the two strands of moral thinking in a variety of ways. Let us begin with a reflection on how norms are experienced. When we act morally we feel that we "must" do what is required of us in the situation. Philosophers call this feeling "practical necessity". It is a feeling that we "ought" to act in a certain way. It is an internal feeling of pressure or strong motivation towards an action even in the presence of contrary inclinations or desires. So an honest person, in a situation when it would be to their advantage to tell a lie and when they feel some temptation to do so, will also feel some pressure towards telling the truth. Again, confronted with an opportunity to gain a great advantage by killing someone, a moral person will feel it impossible to do so.

An ethics of duty conceives of the nature of this practical necessity as a feeling that we must act from duty. Kant calls it "respect for the moral law". It is our duty to tell the truth or to preserve the life of an innocent human being. Our duty is what we are commanded to do by morality. The notion of the Ten Commandments is telling. Here our duties are literally conceived of as commands. In the natural law tradition, the command is less direct since it issues from our nature as human beings, but, once again, it is our nature as created by God that gives normativity to this command: that is, that makes it obligatory for us. In Kant's theory of morality, man's reason gives him the moral law, which he then obeys. And utilitarians argue that we have an impartial obligation to pursue the greatest happiness for the greatest number. In all of these theories, the characteristic stance of the human agent in relation to the demands of morality is that of obedience. The moral law is conceived of as existing over and above us, in some sense, and our duty is to obey it. So the feeling that we "must" do something in a morally difficult situation arises from our sense of ourselves as having to *obey* a moral law or *follow* a moral principle.

One form that this obedience can take in everyday life is deductive thinking. Duty ethics is a form of moral thinking that is based on principles. To base one's ethical thinking on principles is to approach moral problems by asking what moral law, general norm or principle might apply to it. So if there is a situation in which I might gain an advantage by telling a lie, I might bring to mind the principle that lying is wrong and come to see that I should not tell that lie. If I were of a theoretical frame of mind I might also ask why the principle that lying is wrong is binding upon me and this might lead me to ask whether there is a more general principle of which the principle that forbids lying is an application, whether it be "fulfil the tendencies that are inherent in human nature", "do not do what it would be rationally inconsistent to want everyone to do" or "do whatever normally leads to the greatest benefit of the greatest number". In this way our practical lives become a logical expression of a rational system of principles. Even if not every individual agent goes through such an explicit set of rational thought processes on every occasion in which a decision is called for, their decision could be seen to be rational and therefore moral if such a logical process could be reconstructed in order to justify their decision. The two salient features of this model are first that decision-making is a rational, deductive process unaffected by emotion or the agent's own interests, and secondly that the decisions are derived from general principles for which a rational foundation can be offered, if not by the agent herself then certainly by moral theorists generally. In short, to do the right thing is to obey the moral law or follow a moral principle.

In contrast, virtue ethics conceives of the virtuous agent as *wanting* to do what morality requires. Because of the character traits that she has, an honest person will want to tell the truth. Even in situations where she may also feel a contrary desire to tell a lie because it would be to her advantage to do so, she will feel a desire to tell the truth. We may suppose that she feels this desire because she sees herself as an honest person and she wants to maintain that image of herself or because, as I put it earlier, she loves the truth. Rather than feeling herself bound by a moral requirement with which she does not identify and which she therefore has to obey in the way that she might obey an external command, she feels internally motivated to tell the truth because of her honest character.

> A *virtue* is a good quality of character, more specifically a disposition to respond to, or acknowledge, items within its field or fields in an excellent or good enough way.   Christine Swanton, *Virtue Ethics: A Pluralist View*, 19

Another way of developing this contrast is to say that whereas duty ethics conceives of moral motivation or practical necessity as obedience to rules, virtue ethics conceives of moral motivation or practical necessity as responsiveness to values. An honest person values truth and if she finds herself in a situation where she might tell the truth or tell a lie to advantage herself, she will respond to the value that the truth holds for her. If "truth" is too abstract a concept to serve as the object of love or commitment in this account, we might want to consider "honour" as the relevant value. An honest person will consider it dishonourable to lie and will be motivated not to lie by a sense of honour. Again, a virtuous person will value knowledge and will respond to that value by being curious and open minded and by seeking to overcome ignorance and deception. To have this attitude is another form of loving the truth. Whatever in the world has value will be acknowledged and responded to appropriately by a virtuous person. Rather than feeling that such a response has the form of obedience in relation to a command, it will be felt as a love for the relevant value: a love that issues in responsive action.

Here is yet another way of explaining how a virtuous agent comes to want to do what is virtuous. Whereas duty ethics would urge such an agent to follow moral principles when she is in doubt as to what to do in a given situation, virtue ethics suggests that agents are guided not only by moral principles but also by what other virtuous agents do. When seeking to understand what should be done in a particular situation, a moral agent might ask what a virtuous person would do. A virtuous person becomes an example to be followed and a source of moral guidance. Such an example may be someone who is a personal acquaintance such as a parent, or an impressive colleague at work, or it may be someone who is known from history such as Jesus, Mahatma Gandhi or Nelson Mandela. The question that a virtue ethicist asks in situations of moral complexity is not "What general principle applies here?" but "What would a virtuous person do in this situation?" In a situation in which we might be tempted to tell a lie, we might make the judgement that, because Judy is an honest person in that she usually avoids telling lies, to understand what it is to be honest in a specific circumstance we need only look to Judy. We might ask what Judy would do. The question we are asking when we look for guidance is not why lying as such is wrong, but why we should not tell a lie in a situation in which an honest person would not tell one. And the answer to this question is not always found in some rational argument but in the exemplary nature of a virtuous person. It is because the exemplary person is inspirational, impressive and admirable that the norm she instantiates is impressed upon us as a norm to be followed. Rather than being convinced by rational argument to respect that value, we are inspired to adopt it by impressive examples. This is why practical necessity is experienced by a virtuous agent as a desire to do what would be virtuous rather than as obedience to a principle.

II

Duty ethics conceives of norms as absolutely binding. It is not a matter of doing your duty because you feel like it. Duties do not come in degrees of stringency measured by the intensity of the agent's commitment to them. Duties are binding no matter how you feel and no matter what the circumstances are. But this can lead to situations of moral conflict. What if two absolute duties conflict? The answer is that if you fail to obey a moral command it must be for a good moral reason. The only thing that could relieve you of the obligation to return a borrowed book would be if you had another more important obligation. So if you were on the way to return the borrowed book and saw a child struggling in the river and you were a good swimmer, you would have an obligation to save the child even if, in doing so, the book ended up in the water and was thus all but destroyed. Even though you cannot now return the borrowed book, you will still have done the right thing because you fulfilled a more important duty – that of saving a human life – than the duty of returning the borrowed book. Many duty ethicists say that a duty, while absolute in the sense that it is objective and binding for everyone, is also *prima facie*. This means that, on the face of it, we have such a duty, but if other more important duties arise it can be cancelled out. And if it can be cancelled out in this way, then it disappears and has no hold on us at all. When you destroyed the borrowed book while saving the drowning child, you did the right thing. The more important duty cancelled out the less important one so that, in that situation, you no longer had an obligation to return the book. Accordingly, there is no need to regret that you destroyed the borrowed book.

In contrast, virtue ethics considers duties from the agent's point of view and allows the agent to judge their stringency. It is certainly courageous of you to have saved the child and it was certainly honourable of you to have wanted to return the borrowed book. Given that you could not do both, and given that you were a person of good character, it was appropriate for you to have followed your intuitive feeling that saving the child was more important. But returning the book does not cease to be important as well. It follows that it is also appropriate for you to regret having destroyed the book even as you congratulate yourself on saving the child. Although you acted courageously in saving the child, you also express your virtue by regretting the loss of the book and trying to make it up to its owner. There has been a moral cost in your action, however admirable it was, and a virtuous person acknowledges that cost. It has not been obliterated by a formal calculus of absolute, *prima facie* duties that decrees that the only thing you had a duty to do was to save the child. In this way, the obligations that a virtuous agent might feel can vary in stringency. It will be a part of your virtue not only that you are committed to moral values, but also that you can make the judgement as to which value is the more important. Further, it expresses your virtue that you feel you have to do something to make things right if a less stringent moral requirement cannot be fulfilled in a particular situation.

> If a genuinely tragic dilemma is what a virtuous agent emerges from, it will be the case that she emerges having done a terrible thing, the very sort of thing that the callous, dishonest, unjust, or in general vicious agent would characteristically do – killed someone, or let them die, betrayed a trust, violated someone's serious rights. And hence it will not be possible to say that she has acted well. What follows from this is not the impossibility of virtue but the possibility of some situations from which even a virtuous agent cannot emerge with her life unmarred.   Rosalind Hursthouse, *On Virtue Ethics*, 74

III

The ethics of duty is universal in form. It is apt to say that whatever duty applies to any individual will apply to everyone universally if it is a genuine moral duty. If it is wrong to lie in this particular situation, it is always wrong to lie. We can also put the point the other way around. Given the deductive conception of practical reason typical of duty ethics, if it is wrong for anyone to lie it must be wrong for me to lie in this situation as well. Lying is always *prima facie* wrong.

In contrast, because virtue ethics envisages individuals responding to morally salient situations from out of their well-formed characters, the focus is upon the particularity of those situations. The individual is not described as applying a general principle, but as responding to the particular case. This position has been called "particularism". It is well illustrated by the people of the French village of Le Chambon, who courageously and generously sheltered fleeing Jewish refugees during the Second World War. They did so as a simple and direct response to a perceived need in a concrete situation. There are no reports of the villagers consulting general principles or deducing their duties from universal norms. Even the village pastor took the simple and direct approach, expressive of his Christian commitment, of helping the refugees because they just happened to show up looking for help. The villagers felt pangs of sympathy for the persecuted, saw that there was something they could do to help, and were motivated to do it. There is no doubt that these actions could be justified rationally on the basis of moral principles, but the reports of the events do not record anyone referring to such principles in order to generate a sense of obligation.

> The villagers were greatly perplexed at the notion that there was anything particularly worthy of note, much less of extraordinary praise, in sheltering persons whose lives were in danger.
> Lawrence A. Blum, *Moral Perception and Particularity*, 91–2

Particularism is a theory of morality that is discussed as much by duty ethicists as it is by virtue ethicists, although my argument here is that it is most at home in virtue ethics. It disputes the claim that moral duties are ever to be articulated in general form. The very fact that moral dilemmas show these duties to be *prima facie* shows that they are not universally binding. A moral agent always has to judge what she is to do in a particular context and with an eye to the particular circumstances of that context. If I am asked by a would-be murderer where the axe that he has lent me is, I am morally permitted to lie to him and also to not return what he has lent me. I need to make a judgement sensitive to the specifics of the situation. For many moral theorists this implies that moral principles should be thought of as generalizations drawn by induction from the past moral decisions of individuals and from impressive exemplars, rather than as pre-existing norms from which we deduce what we should do. They act as guides for our actions because they encapsulate the acquired and revisable wisdom of our ethical traditions.

The virtue ethicist agrees with these points because they point to the importance of particular judgement in specific situations, the relative unimportance of moral principles conceived as absolute and universal norms, the significance of exemplary figures, and the need to be sensitive to what is morally salient in specific circumstances. Such sensitivity will be an expression of the virtuous character and emotional make-up of ethical agents.

A decision to act, especially in morally difficult situations, is always a creative leap in the dark. There are always features in the situation that are unique to that situation. Each individual who can be affected by your decision is a unique person enmeshed in a unique set of relationships with one another and with you. Accordingly, your decision to act goes beyond what could be given in general principles or norms. Such principles or norms are always articulated with a degree of abstraction. They need to be in order to be widely applicable. But your situation is both specific and rich in detail. Accordingly, you cannot just deduce what you should do from a general principle. You have to take the particularities of the situation into account. You have to take the needs and the background of each affected individual into account. It follows that a general principle or norm is only a general guide or a rule of thumb. It will not dictate to you what you should do in any detail. You have to form your own judgement and this judgement will go beyond what the principle alone says to you. Accordingly, the decision you make will not be entirely dictated by the norm; it will also be expressive of your judgement, your experience, your character and your virtue. And it will be a risk. You could be assured that you have done the right thing if you could just deduce your decision from a principle. But you cannot do so. Therefore you take a risk whenever you make a difficult decision. You put yourself on the line. You make a commitment. You take responsibility.

This last is an important point. If it were true that we could just deduce our decisions from general principles or act merely in obedience to moral laws, then we could assign the responsibility for our actions to those principles or laws. We could say, in a sense, that we were just following orders. The "orders" may have come from moral norms, but it would still be valid to think that we were not fully responsible for our actions. If we deduced our decisions on the basis of logic alone, then we could only have an attenuated sense of responsibility for our actions. But we are fully responsible. And the reason we are responsible is that we have had to make a judgement about the specific situation, about all the people and other values in that situation, about what other admirable people may have done in similar situations, and about the norms and principles that might apply to it. Our decision will be a declaration of where we stand on the matter at hand. If I decide not to lie, I shall be making a leap of faith that, in this situation, being truthful was the best thing to do. I shall be declaring myself as truthful and committing myself to the value of truth in such situations as this. Nothing guarantees that this will have been the best option to take and subsequent reflection may lead me to revise my judgement. That is the risk I take when I take responsibility for my decision. It is the accumulation of decisions, understood in this rich sense of taking risks and committing myself to moral values, that constitutes my character as it shapes itself through my life. Virtue ethics acknowledges the moral ambiguity of many issues and situations. In morally complex situations you cannot always know for certain that what you decide to do would be the right course of action. You simply have to decide, make that leap of faith, and take responsibility.

IV

Another contrast between the ethics of duty and virtue ethics is between the stress on reason that is typical of the former and the recognition that the latter gives to our emotions. The clearest example of this contrast is found in Kant. For him our moral thinking must not only be rational, but it must be based on *a priori* reason: that is, thinking that is purely formal and completely devoid of any emotion, interest or inclination. In this conception of reason the only criterion for correctness is logical consistency rather than sensitivity to what might be felt to be important in a situation or feelings towards people involved in it. The thinking that grounds our norms must be the thinking engaged in by an imagined "perfectly rational being": that is, a being not motivated by any wants, desires, emotions or affective ties to anything or anyone else. Even the emotion of love for others is deemed by Kant to be a distraction from the clear-headed thinking that establishes what it is our duty to do.

In contrast, virtue ethics applauds positive emotions. In speaking of character in "Moral terminology" §II, I understood character as including behavioural dispositions to action and hidden motivators of action that are either imprinted in our genes or developed through our upbringing, or both. But besides dispositions to action, character also includes attitudes, feelings and value commitments such as thoughtfulness and sentiments of care, love and concern. These last three are emotions. Sometimes an emotion will be an expression of character, as when we say that James is saddened by the suffering of others because he is a caring person. And sometimes an emotion will give rise to an action, as when we say that James was so upset when hearing of the plight of the homeless that he gave money to a charity committed to looking after them. Further, this action will reinforce James's character as a caring person. In this way emotion is part of the dynamic link that connects character and behaviour. James may well also give thought to these matters and judge that giving to this charity is a good thing to do, or even an obligatory thing to do, but it is difficult to see how this thought would motivate him to act if he did not also feel the emotion of caring for the homeless. Moreover, he might not give thought to what he should do if he were not initially moved by emotion. Emotions or "moral sentiments" that are especially relevant to virtue ethics include feelings of benevolence towards others, sympathy for the suffering of others, concern about the prospects of future generations, a sense of justice in relation to peoples in the third world and caring about loved ones.

V

This mention of emotion, especially the emotion of caring, brings to mind a debate that has been raging in moral theory for some years.

While studying the moral development of children, the psychologist Carol Gilligan discovered that girls often approach moral issues differently from boys. In schoolyard disputes, boys will insist on following rules and receiving what is theirs by right, whereas girls try to resolve differences through compromise so as to maintain friendly relationships. Gilligan referred to these approaches as a "justice perspective" and a "caring perspective" respectively. Although she did not insist that these perspectives were confined exclusively to boys and girls respectively, she did suggest that, as previous research had been done largely with boys, the picture of morality that had emerged placed too much stress on an ethics based on rules, rights and the pursuit of justice at the expense of an acknowledgement of caring and the importance of interpersonal relationships. It will be immediately clear that this distinction echoes the one I am mapping between an ethics of duty and an ethics of virtue. The ethics of duty highlights rules and obligations and the doing of the right thing, whereas virtue ethics acknowledges the importance of emotions, including interpersonal feelings of caring and affection.

VI

This point highlights another important difference between the justice perspective of the ethics of duty and the caring perspective of virtue ethics. Our duties are said to be impartial. If I have a duty to help those in need whom I can help, I have that duty in respect of anyone who is in need and whom I can help. Classical utilitarians illustrate this by drawing a scenario in which there are two people in a burning building and you can only save one of them. One of them is a great scientist who can bring much benefit to the world while the other is your aged mother. Although some contemporary utilitarians moderate this view, the impartialist thinking advocated by this form of duty ethics would say that it is your duty to save the scientist because he can bring great benefit to the world while your mother cannot do so. The fact that you have a close and emotional relationship to your mother is deemed to be irrelevant because to be influenced by it would make your thinking partial. You would be placing your own preference – based on whom you care about – above the good conceived from a position of impartial reason. Virtue ethics on the other hand, in so far as it embraces the caring perspective, finds no difficulty in admiring you if you save your mother and let the scientist burn (although it would also be virtuous to regret your inability to save him). A virtuous person is admired when she is appropriately partial in acknowledging the web of interpersonal relationships of which she is a part.

VII

In order to understand the importance of acknowledging the emotions in practical judgements more fully, I need to distinguish what has been called "reasons externalism" from "reasons internalism". The former position is espoused by many duty ethicists, whereas most virtue ethicists assume the latter. Reasons externalism says that situations in the world, including moral and social norms, can be reasons for people to act in certain ways. If a given society, or the human species as such, holds to the principle that murder is wrong and can justify this principle with some rational argument, then that norm is a reason for any agent to adhere to it. This is called "externalism" because it does not depend on what any given agent thinks or feels about it. If you are a criminal considering whether you might kill someone who stands in the way of some nefarious scheme that you are hatching, you might not have given any thought to the principle that murder is wrong. You might be thinking only of the advantage you may gain by killing your rival. However, even though you are not thinking about that principle and even though, because of your bad upbringing, you have not internalized it, it still is a norm or a reason that applies to you. But because it is not a content of your thinking or your character, it is an "external" reason. The norm exists in society and it applies to you whatever your own view might be.

An even more striking example of an external reason – although not an example of one that has moral significance – is the following scenario. You are walking to the railway station to catch the 8.30 train. You do this every day so you know how long the walk takes and how fast you should be walking. However, unbeknown to you, a timetable change has occurred for the train and it is now due to leave at 8.28. At your current pace you will miss the train. It follows that you have a reason to hurry. But, of course, in so far as you do not know about the change in the timetable you do not do so. The reason applies to you but you do not act on it. Notice that this situation is described in terms of your "having" a reason, or in terms of "there being" a reason for you to act, even though no such reason is being entertained by you in your thinking. These reasons are "external" to you.

They are also very puzzling as "reasons". Why would we use the word "reason" for a situation that you are not aware of? Very often, when we speak of "reasons" we are talking about thoughts or feelings that people have that motivate them to do something. If another passenger who knows of the timetable change asks you why you are not hurrying to the station you would say "because the train is due to leave at 8.30". This is the content of your thinking. It is not true, but it is your view of the matter. You can only be motivated to act by the view that you have rather than by the fact of the matter if you do not know that fact. This is the position of the "reasons internalist". It is the view that a reason is only a reason if it is present in the thinking or feeling of the agent. To be a reason, a consideration has to relate to an internal state of the agent. It need not be an explicit thought. It might be some desire the agent has. In this sense you do "have" a reason to hurry to the station, but this is because you have a desire to catch the train. This reason is not given by the fact of the train's being early; it is expressive of your desire. For a reasons internalist, a reason to do something is a motivation to do it. It is an internal state of the agent. It makes no sense to refer to a state of affairs that the agent does not know about or to a norm that the agent has not internalized as a reason the agent "has" if that reason plays no role in the motivational structure of that agent. To have a reason is not just to be in a situation to which it would be prudent or moral to respond; it is to be motivated to recognize that you are in such a situation and to feel the call of that situation upon you. And you would feel this call in one case because you wanted to catch the train, and in the other case because you had a conviction that murder is wrong. What is needed for a consideration to operate as a reason is that there must be something in your character that would motivate you to respond to it practically. Being a practical reason, it must generate some degree of "practical necessity". The importance of this distinction between external and internal reasons is that it points, once again, to the agent's character as central to any description of moral agency from the virtue ethics perspective.

This distinction also solves a problem that many moral theorists in the tradition of duty ethics have found puzzling. This problem is that of linking moral thinking to moral action. It is one thing to conclude from principles that a particular action should be done and quite another to be motivated to do it. Or so it is said. If you distinguish reason from desire and motivation then you might indeed suggest that you could rationally come to see that an action was the right one to perform without also being moved to do it. Reasons externalism makes it inevitable that there will be a gap between there being a reason for you to do something – even if you recognize that reason in pure thought – and your actually wanting to do it. In contrast, if even your thinking is an expression of character and is motivated by the same virtuous motivations that motivate your actions, then your judgement that an action is the right one to perform will also at the same time be a decision to perform it if the circumstances call for it. Your reason will be a motivation. If, perchance, you do not perform the action the problem will be one of "weakness of will" rather than of there being a gap between the putative faculty of reason and the putative faculty of motivation. And "weakness of will" is the lack of a virtue such as that of courage, wholeheartedness, determination, fortitude or persistence.

VIII

The distinction between reasons externalism and reasons internalism also calls into question the view of many duty ethicists that morality exists somehow over against us as something that we are obliged to obey and that moral theorists can define on the basis of pure rationality or metaphysics. This view has been variously called "moral realism", "moral objectivism" or "moral cognitivism". It begins with the basic point that, in ordinary language, we say things such as "It is wrong to steal". If this statement is true, and if one adheres to a correspondence theory of truth or a reference theory of meaning, then there must be a "moral fact" to which this statement corresponds by describing it correctly. This moral fact is the fact that stealing is wrong. Just as the new train timetable gives you a reason to hurry, this moral fact provides you with a reason not to steal whether or not you are aware of it. Irrespective of your attitude to stealing, it is wrong for you to steal because of the fact that stealing is wrong. Moral realism of this sort goes back at least as far as Plato, for whom the idea of Goodness was a reality that existed objectively outside our own world so that our knowledge of it would move us to act virtuously. When Plato suggests, through Socrates, that knowledge is virtue he does not just mean that it is an ethically good thing to be knowledgeable; he means that our knowledge of what the reality of moral goodness is will make us virtuous. But in attributing an objective reality to Goodness and other values he also inaugurated that tradition of philosophy in which it became the task of detached and theoretical thought to discover these realities and to describe them for the benefit of ordinary folk who did not have the theoretical sophistication to discover them for themselves. As Socrates argues, for most people their immersion in bodily desires and concerns prevents them from discerning the pure and absolute realities that should influence their lives. Despite Plato's mention of virtue, he was a moral realist.

In contrast, the tradition of virtue ethics is more inclined to suggest that if morality exists, it exists within us. We are brought up into it. It is always already there in our lives in one form or another. And because of this we will respond, or be motivated to respond, ethically to situations that we see as calling for such a response. Our judgement as to what a situation calls upon us to do will be an expression of our characters and a response to what is ethically salient in the situation before us, rather than a conclusion drawn deductively from "external reasons" that moral theorists will see as applying to us.

If the question is raised as to whether our ethical ideals and moral norms are "real" and objective as opposed to merely matters of subjective opinion, then I would say that this is a false dilemma. Theories of the social construction of reality that stem from sociology would suggest that morality can exist in the characters of virtuous individuals without thereby being merely subjective. Although not all virtue ethicists would agree with me on this point (and most duty ethicists certainly would not), I would argue that morality does not have to be a reality that exists outside human experience in order to be objective. One example to briefly illustrate how this would work would be money. Take a one-dollar banknote. What is it in reality? You could answer this by saying that it is a piece of paper with printed marks on it. This is what it is as a physical object. But it is also a medium of exchange and, as such, it has a value in a system of exchange. You would not roll it up to use as doorstop in the way you could use a piece of notepaper. It "really" is money. It is a "fact" that it has a definite monetary value. But on what is this fact based? It would seem to be based on a number of economic conventions and institutions. In the absence of these it would just be a piece of paper. If after some world cataclysm we returned to a primitive life of exchange and barter without money, such a banknote would have no value and it would no longer be money. So the "reality" of money is a reality that is established by human conventions and arrangements. This reality is part of the context in which we live and we do not question it. It would seem absurd to destroy dollar banknotes. But this reality is not based on any metaphysical reality that is beyond our everyday world. It is not established by pure theory. It is established by, and lasts only as long as, the implicit acceptance of the relevant conventions on the part of people generally.

I suggest that morality is "real" in just this sense. Its reality does not arise from metaphysical or universal realities or from pure reason; it arises from convention. All well-meaning people would agree that stealing is wrong and would not even think about stealing something of considerable value. But this is not because to do so accords with some principle that arises from a reality beyond that of this world. It is because of a well-ingrained convention. One might add that it is a very rational convention in that any society that tried to live by a different one would not survive as a society, but this only shows that the social construction of morality has produced those norms that are most conducive to the survival of society and of individuals within it. That there is nothing necessary or inevitable about this is shown by the many conventions that are followed with the same seriousness as morality but that are obviously arbitrary. Why should Sunday be the Sabbath? Why not rather Tuesday? Why should we show respect to others by bowing: why not give them the thumbs-up? Why is homosexuality thought to be immoral by so many?

That our social and moral conventions are an important matter even if they do not have metaphysical or *a priori* foundations is illustrated by one of the central tenets of duty ethics: that all men are created equal. This proposition was put forward as so certain as to be self-evident. And yet it is far from evident. Look around you and you will see people who are unequal in respect of many important features: features such as their wealth, their health, their talents, their gender, their race, their religious and moral beliefs and their nationality. In the past, if you were born to an aristocratic family you had higher status and more legal rights than if you were born to a peasant family. Empirically speaking, human beings are not all equal. How is it then that we take as self-evident that they are equal? It is because during our history we have gradually developed the concept of the rule of law and along with it the idea that everyone has equal status before the law. Like money, this is a human convention, but one that has become so ingrained and so important to us that we take it to be self-evident. Peoples with a different history do not see it as self-evident. As a consequence, some moral theorists attempt to develop theories that suggest that we are equal not because we have constructed the concept of a person with equal moral rights in the course of our specific history, but because we are all created by God or because all rational beings have equal dignity as founders of the moral law. The question that this raises is whether the reality of our legal and moral equality is founded upon such theories or whether it emerges from human history. Virtue ethics can be comfortable with the latter suggestion.

The basis of norms

I

I have just suggested that the ethics of duty bases its moral norms on what I called "metaphysical or *a priori* reasons". I now need to explore this further. I have already mentioned the Ten Commandments as an example of a divine command theory, which suggests that the basis of moral principles is the command of God. The natural law tradition appeals to a divinely created human nature to suggest that we are obliged to fulfil the tendencies in that human nature. Kant's moral theory posits human freedom and human rationality as the basis for the imperatives that constitute our morality. And utilitarianism suggests that we are obliged to do whatever leads to the greatest happiness for the greater number. In all but the last of these, the basis for moral norms could be described as "metaphysical". What I mean by this is that some purely theoretical concept or other-worldly entity is appealed to in order to ground our duties. This is most obvious in the divine command theory and in the religious version of natural law theory, where it is God who is seen as the origin of the universal and absolute authority of morality. The pure reason upon which Kantian moral theory wants to base moral norms also attempts to delineate a sphere of thinking that abstracts from specific historical and social contexts in order to show that norms are universally binding in themselves. But even in Kant, for morality to have a purpose requires that we conceive of God as the source of our ultimate reward. Moreover, *a priori* reason is postulated as being an expression of free will in so far as it is removed from all influences of the emotions or inclinations that arise from our actual, situated existence in the world. In this way the metaphysical or purely theoretical concept of free will is among the bases of the normativity of our duties. Utilitarianism aims to be a "naturalistic" doctrine in that it does not appeal to any metaphysical postulations. But it is precisely because it does not appeal to some such basis that utilitarianism can be criticized by suggesting that anyone who does not care about other people would not feel obliged to ensure that their actions led to the greatest happiness for the greatest number. It is difficult to see what would convince us to care impartially about the welfare of others if we were not already inclined to do so. Perhaps utilitarianism is actually based on the virtue of caring.

In contrast to this tendency of most theories of duty ethics to appeal to metaphysical doctrines, virtue ethics bases itself firmly on actual life as it is lived and on the actual intuitions of human beings living in actual communities and historical epochs. The judgement of most people as to what is virtuous and the values that people of good character admire are quite adequately based on such intuitions. In relation to the norm against telling lies, for example, the intuitions of well-brought-up people would suggest that, given that we want to get on with each other and have orderly social arrangements that we can rely on, it is a good idea to tell the truth unless there is a better reason not to do so. You do not have to engage in metaphysics to see that.

Virtue ethics sees these common-sense intuitions as expressions of the moral sentiments and practical reason of agents of good character as shaped by the traditions of the communities in which those agents live. By "tradition" I mean the collective wisdom of a people as handed down through upbringing and education in a given community. It is the basis of the moral intuitions that people give expression to when they engage in moral theory as well as when they make moral decisions. Traditions are shaped by many cultural and historical influences, including moral theory itself. One very important way in which a tradition is formed and handed on is by allusion to exemplary figures or events from the history of that tradition: events such as successful revolutions or wars of independence, and figures such as leaders in such struggles, or the founders of religions. Over time, in any given community, the examples of exemplary figures accumulate and ground a generally held understanding of what it is to act virtuously. Upbringing and education then pass this understanding on to further generations who further shape the tradition as they respond to new situations and moral challenges. It is from the background of common-sense intuitions shaped by tradition in this way that a virtuous agent will be able to respond appropriately to the morally difficult aspects of a specific situation. And those responses in turn will further shape the traditions of which they were the expression.

It has to be admitted that the concept of tradition has become problematic today. In modern societies tradition has less of a hold on us than used to be the case in the past. We tend to think we can, or need to, think through every situation for ourselves. The Enlightenment has taught us to be distrustful of traditions, especially if they are religious. However, no one is an island and we cannot escape being shaped by tradition. Moreover, in pluralist societies we are shaped by a variety of traditions. We might be shaped by our ethnic group's history, by the history of our nation, by our religion, by the school we went to and by the associations we have been a part of. Moreover, we are affected by advertising and by the myriad influences upon us that arise in contemporary post-industrial societies. More negatively, our caring and moral sentiments may come under challenge from the competitiveness, indifference to others and envy that modern life encourages. As well, our common-sense intuitions can be naive or confused. People may hold incompatible moral beliefs: for example, that no one should suffer unjustly, but also that people who are strangers to us have less of a call on our moral concern. These are just some of the reasons why moral theory is needed. But my point is that the intuitions that arise from tradition continue to constitute the context in which such theory is engaged in. To appeal to metaphysics or *a priori* reason in an attempt to escape from such a context into a realm of absolute and universal objectivity is to create a discourse that departs from ordinary life and that appeals to arguments that people other than moral theorists will not be able to readily understand or agree on.

II

There is a more formal way of putting this last point. Using technical terms we might say that the ethics of duty is very often "foundationalist", whereas virtue ethics takes a "hermeneutic" approach. To say of a theory that it is foundationalist is to suggest that it seeks to establish the basis or foundation of what that theory is about. In the theory of knowledge, for example, a question that is often asked is whether our knowledge can be based upon clear and indubitable insights. Empiricists argue that sense experience provides such a basis, whereas Descartes famously suggested that the one and only indubitable proposition is "I think, therefore I am". It was on the foundation of such a proposition that Descartes went on to try to establish everything that we can know. Accordingly, Descartes's epistemology is an example of foundationalism. Traditionally, moral theory has been foundationalist in this sense and has sought to uncover or posit the foundations of our moral obligations. Such foundations needed to be objective, absolute and universal in order to provide the basis for our system of morality. Moral judgements were said to be grounded in a "view from nowhere" rather than being based on the perspective of any particular individual or group. This is why they appeal to metaphysical or *a priori* foundations and also why they use only thin concepts.

The "hermeneutic" approach contrasts with this in that it does not seek to ground moral obligation in any foundation outside the practice of morality. It begins by suggesting that our moral judgements are interpretations that use thick concepts based on attitudes that we already have. So, for example, if I judge that Horatio's action in defending the bridge against the invading army is courageous it is because I already have a number of attitudes relevant to that situation. I already regard the invading army as unjustified in their attack and regard the city that Horatio is defending as worthy of such defence. Moreover, I already have the concept of courage and, in particular, I am able to distinguish it from foolhardiness. After all, given the overwhelming odds that Horatio is facing it would be easy to call him foolhardy. I call him courageous because I share or at least appreciate his commitment to the defence of his city. So to interpret his action as courageous as opposed to foolhardy requires my having the thick concept of courage and also my sharing some of Horatio's attitudes. There is not some neutral or value-free point of view from which I can make that judgement. There is not some absolute or foundational value or standard of behaviour that exists in itself and that can be applied objectively to this situation. I am myself involved in the situation even though I am an observer of it far removed in space and time. I have an attitude to Horatio's cause and his action. I simply could not understand Horatio if I did not imagine myself into his context. Such a judgement is not objective.

But this inevitable lack of objectivity is even more profound. Not only do I need some implicit understanding of what courage is in order to make the judgement that Horatio was courageous, but I need to be courageous myself to some degree to make that judgement. A coward would see Horatio's action as foolhardy. It would be an action that such a person could not relate to or identify with. If I see it as courageous it is because, to some extent, I can identify with it. I share, not just Horatio's attitudes, but also his courage in the sense that I could imagine myself wanting to act in a similar way. Take another example. Imagine yourself as a tourist visiting a Buddhist temple in a foreign country. Not being a Buddhist you have no understanding of the meaning of the statues and decorations. Now some other tourists come in. They are smoking and talking loudly and photographing everything around them, including some local worshippers. In short they are acting boorishly. Now, if you were boorish yourself you would not notice this. You would regard their behaviour as unremarkable. But if you have the virtue of reverence and are sensitive both to the beauty and the religious significance of that place, then you will see their behaviour as boorish and, possibly, be embarrassed on their behalf. Once again, it is clear that this reaction is not objective. But my point is that it is a reaction that already expresses the virtue the lack of which it sees in those other tourists. So you need to have the virtue in order to recognize it and make judgements about it. Complete cowards would not even recognize themselves as cowards but would deceive themselves into thinking that they were, for example, prudent. They would have to have some glimmer of courage in their characters to even upbraid themselves for being cowardly. There is no objective, rational foundation from which such judgements can be made. Whereas all you need in order to make a correct judgement or a decision about duty is to be rational, to make an appropriate judgement about virtue requires you to be virtuous. This shows that such judgements are not foundational. I must *already* have an understanding of what courage is and an appreciation of the importance of courage in order to judge that Horatio is admirable.

Moreover, the understanding that I have of what courage is comes from making judgements of this kind. It is not that I have been given some objective or absolute definition of courage and have then applied it successfully to particular cases. Rather, when I was a child I experienced the actions of others or stories about them and other people called them examples of courage and, when asked, explained to me why. Sometimes, older people called certain actions foolhardy, sometimes they described them as courageous, and sometimes as heroic. Sometimes I have done things myself that have earned the description "courageous". From these cases, from reflection, from literature and from the movies, I have come to learn what courage is. There is not some canonical dictionary definition that names the essence of courage or courage as a thing-in-itself. There is just the way courage is talked about and agreed upon by people. As I grow up, I begin to share this communal understanding embedded in the way we use the relevant words. Even if I am hard put to give a clear definition of courage, I may use the word and its related concepts perfectly well in ordinary language and recognize instances of it in the world around me. Without a clear knowledge of the essence of what courage is, my thinking is not foundational. I do not know exactly what makes an action courageous. But I can make the relevant judgements and I do so from out of an implicit background understanding. In turn, my particular judgements and my own actions contribute to that background understanding. Every time I experience an act of courage in all its uniqueness and particularity, in myself or in others, it contributes to my general understanding of what courage is. In this way my thinking is circular. It stays within what has been called a "hermeneutic circle". I need an appreciative understanding to make the judgements, and my judgements contribute to my evolving understanding of, and my commitment to, that virtue.

Because so many philosophers think in foundationalist ways, they find this circularity uncomfortable. Yet there is nothing mysterious about it. Imagine you are reading a book and you come across a word that you do not understand. You look it up in a dictionary. But what the dictionary gives you is another word or set of words. Of course, it is hoped that you will understand those words, but if you do not then you can look them up as well until you find words that you do understand. In this way, it is the grasp of the English language that you already have that is being appealed to in order to help you understand particular words or phrases. And your grasp of the English language consists in, and is added to by, your understanding of particular words or phrases. Even if the case were one where you were reading a German text and you were looking up a word in an English–German dictionary, your understanding of the unfamiliar German word would depend upon your already having a grasp of the relevant English words. So your being able to operate with language depends upon your already having a grasp of language with which you then make individual judgements as to what words mean, and these individual judgements contribute to your overall understanding of the language.

And there is a further point. When you look up a word in the dictionary and are given other words or phrases that are synonyms for the word you were looking up, the basis of the meanings of those word or phrases is how other people use those words. The dictionary does not tell you how a word connects with what it refers to. It tells you how it connects with other words and how other people use those words. It is the actual usage of words by the linguistic community that establishes the meaning of words rather than their connection to realities that exist outside language. At no point can you break out of the circle of language and show that a word means what it does because it has some inevitable or necessary connection with reality. Why does the English word "house" refer to a specific range of buildings? What is it about that spelling or that sound that links it to such buildings? If there were such a necessary link how is it that other languages use different words? The only way to ensure that you are using the right word to express an idea or convey some information is to note the way that others who are known to be competent users of the language use that word. And how do we know that those others are using the right word? Because its being the right word is based on the fact that they – persons who are known as competent users of the language – are using it. This is a circular process in which we are involved all the time. Some philosophers have tried to break out of this circle in order to establish a foundation for language by way of some necessary link between words and what they refer to, but such a project is not necessary for us if we are to use language effectively. We learn language by noting how others use it, by joining in, and by being corrected or encouraged as we do so. By the time we come to wonder how we could become competent in the use of language we already are. And by the time we come to wonder why words have the meanings they have, they already have them.

And so it is with morality. Given the way we are brought up into the ethics of a community, by the time we come to wonder what is right or wrong, and why, we already have ethical convictions and intuitions and we already broadly understand what morality is and what it requires of us. Rather than establish the foundations of morality, our moral thinking cannot but presuppose it. It is not necessary to seek foundations for our morals. If we are in doubt as to what we should do, we simply look to people whom we consider ethically competent and do what they would do or have done. The community gives me my own ethical convictions and intuitions by giving me ethical exemplars. Just as it is unnecessary or even impossible to break out of the circle of language in order to establish the foundations of the meanings of our words, so it is unnecessary or even impossible to break out of the circle of a community's ethics in order to establish the foundations of that ethics.

> The implicit empirical claim that toddlers are taught only the deontologist's rules, not the "thick" concepts, is surely false. Sentences such as "Don't do that, it hurts the cat, you mustn't be cruel", "Be kind to your brother, he's only little", "Don't be so mean, so greedy", are commonly addressed to toddlers. For some reason, we do not seem to teach "just" and "unjust" early on, but we certainly teach "fair" and "unfair".
>
> Rosalind Hursthouse, *On Virtue Ethics*, 38

This is illustrated by how we teach morality to our children. We do not provide foundationalist reasons to our children for the norm that it is wrong to tell lies. We disapprove of them when they do tell lies and we praise them when they are truthful. When we see Judy being truthful in difficult circumstances we say to our own child that that is an example to be followed. Gradually the child learns not only what the word "lie" means, but also that it is something disapproved of. Gradually the child learns to value telling the truth and to feel some practical necessity in favour of telling the truth. The child is entering that circle of thinking and feeling that leads it to want to tell the truth, to admire others who tell the truth, to disapprove of those who tell lies and to consider exemplary truth-tellers as models for its own behaviour. The child is acquiring a good character, and from the perspective of this well-formed character it will regard it as a matter of common sense that lying is wrong. It is in this non-foundationalist and non-justificatory sense that good character is the basis of our norms. To suggest that a person of good character would not do it is to offer a reason or a basis for a norm in the context of a community in which that norm is already widely understood and respected. It would certainly not count as a reason for an outsider who does not share the common sense of that community. But if you were addressing a child or any other new inductee into the community, then it would indeed make sense to say that one should not lie because a virtuous person would not do it. This makes sense within a hermeneutic framework even if it leaves a foundationalist unsatisfied.

I should not leave the impression that it is only virtue ethics that operates within this "hermeneutic circle". Many theorists have recognized that if you do not share the general moral outlook of a group of people, then you will have great difficulty in understanding what they take to be morally serious. If you are not a Muslim, for example, it is very difficult to understand and appreciate the dietary rules associated with Ramadan. Some moral theorists in the tradition of duty ethics speak of "reflective equilibrium", which is a way of thinking about moral issues that is also not foundationalist. It accepts the norms that are part of the common sense of a people and takes the task of moral theory to be to reflect upon those norms and their application so as to ensure clarity and consistency between them. In this way a particular moral decision or policy will be grounded in, and a refinement of, the widely held social consensus on moral norms represented by common sense, rather than any metaphysical or *a priori* rational foundation. The moral intuitions that individuals have and that arise from their socialization into their moral community will be the basis for further thought so as to ensure that they are consistent with that community's norms and are applied appropriately to the situation at hand.

III

The notions of common sense, moral intuition, tradition and community allow me to turn to a problem with virtue ethics that many moral theorists have identified: the problem of relativism. As I mentioned in "The nature of norms" §III, duty ethics conceives of norms as universal. Returning a borrowed book would be an obligation for anyone anywhere: that is, such a duty is an objective or universal obligation not relative to the circumstances or culture of any particular agent. What is morally obligatory or forbidden in one community must be morally obligatory or forbidden in any community. Stealing is wrong anywhere at any time. If there is a practice that is not morally obligatory or forbidden universally, then that practice is relegated to local custom rather than to morality. The reason that the ethics of duty insists on the universality of its norms is that it is foundationalist in its thinking. If it has identified the basis of moral norms either in the commands of the one true God, or in the demands that are requisite for the attainment of the inherent goals of human nature, or in the imperatives that are issued by *a priori* reason, or in the beneficent thinking of impartial individuals anywhere, then those norms must be universal. Such foundations are universally valid.

Although a virtue ethicist would not disagree with this entirely and suggest that many virtues, such as that of being honest, are also universally admired character traits, she would also point to virtues that are relative to specific cultures. Being pious, for example, is a virtue only among people who share religious beliefs. Modesty for women is greatly admired and even enforced in some traditional communities whereas modern secular societies take it less seriously. Moreover, the way in which a particular virtue is conceived and the way it is expressed may differ from culture to culture. For example, in warrior societies, courage will be conceived in terms of how well a warrior stands up to physical danger and injury on the battlefield, whereas in contemporary post-industrial societies, courage might be displayed in the way a person is prepared to jeopardise their career by seeking to expose corporate corruption. Again, if we remember the point that virtue ethics concerns itself with a larger range of activities than just the moral, we might consider that what courtesy requires differs from one culture to another. Sometimes this is merely a matter of varying rules of etiquette, but sometimes it is a matter of attitude. Some cultures expect their heroes to display pride and show disdain for lesser mortals, whereas other cultures urge an egalitarian attitude and the virtue of humility.

In short, virtue ethics accepts that the virtues that are admired by people are very often specific to particular historical and geographical communities. There will be some virtues that it would be hard to imagine not being admired universally: virtues such as honesty, courage and the passion for justice. But that these are so widely admired is a contingent matter and does not depend upon some metaphysical or rational proof that they are valid for everyone. It just happens to be the case that, given the sorts of beings we are and given the sorts of societies we live in, these virtues will be widely admired and people who fail to evince them will be widely despised.

This point has been developed in more theoretical terms by Alasdair MacIntyre. He has argued that because the metaphysical and rational foundations appealed to by most moral theories have lost favour with contemporary thinkers it has become necessary to draw the standards and norms that we are to live by from the communities and practices of which we are a part. I have already stressed how the upbringing and ethical formation that young people receive as they grow into adulthood in specific communities and societies shape their characters in accordance with the ideals and norms that operate in those communities and societies. This is a point that can be confirmed by sociological and psychological studies. The unique contribution that MacIntyre makes to this discussion is his notion of a "practice". A practice is a set of activities structured by social arrangements and centred upon goals that are internal to it. Take, as an example, a profession such as medicine. Medicine is a structured set of activities engaged in by people who are educated and certified to do so in pursuit of goals that are specific to that profession. In the case of medicine these goals centre on the maintenance and restoration of health and the alleviation of suffering resulting from maladies. Notice that these goals are "internal" to the practice. Doctors and other medical workers may also be engaged in their activities in order to gain income and social status, but these goals are not internal to the practice because they are not goals specific to it, whereas curing the sick is. Given these internal goals, specific ways of acting become virtuous within the practice. To be competent in the specific skills associated with doctoring, to keep up with the relevant body of knowledge, to be caring and solicitous towards patients and to feel sympathy for their suffering are all character traits and ways of acting that conduce to the goals of the practice and that improve the manner in which the practice is undertaken. As such they are virtues. The key point is that they are virtues because of what the practice is. They conduce to the goals that are internal to the practice. They are virtues for doctors, although not necessarily exclusive to doctors. In this way virtues are relative to practices.

Once again, we have here an example of the hermeneutic circle. We understand these character traits and ways of behaving as virtues for doctors and medical workers in the context of a wider understanding of the practice of medicine. And our understanding and appreciation of the practice of medicine is enhanced and deepened by our apprehension of doctors who impress us with their virtue.

But there is a problem that is emerging here. A duty theorist might say that it is indeed possible to explain what traits come to be admired as virtues by reference to the practices that people engage in. Such a theorist might agree that virtues can be understood in the context of the practices that they enhance. She might even agree that our virtues are character traits that we have acquired in our upbringing through a process that includes being praised for displaying them. It will be inevitable, given this process, that if we are well brought up we shall acquire those traits that are admired as virtues in our communities. But none of this shows that those virtues are to be morally approved. If I were brought up in a community of thieves and saw myself as committed to the practice of larceny I might well consider that deviousness, disregard for property rights and stealth were virtues that enhanced my practice, conduced to my goals and won the admiration of my family and community. But would this make those traits *moral* virtues? Is stealing not morally wrong? And, if so, would it not follow that all the character traits that conduce to the inherent values and goals of the practice of stealing should be disapproved?

Again, take the point about virtue ethics drawing inspiration from exemplary figures. In the Germany of the 1930s Hitler was an impressive figure to many. He was an inspiration to almost the whole of his nation. Historians describe how many people came to follow him and be impressed by him. But does it follow that they *should* have? Does it follow that they were right to model themselves upon him and to follow his lead? It seems that the appeal to tradition and common sense as the matrix for the moral judgements of virtuous agents leads to the difficulty of relativism. What the Nazis admired as virtue may have been understood with reference to the worldview and traditions of Nazi thought, but it must surely be possible for us to judge those "virtues" and moral stances as having been immoral. That a virtue is judged to be good relative to the common-sense intuitions of the people who are making that judgement does not guarantee that that judgement is correct by the standards that moral theory would endorse from its more metaphysical or purely rational standpoint.

This is a complex issue and one upon which the standing of virtue ethics as a moral theory may be said to stand or fall. The standard objection to relativism in moral theory is that it leaves would-be moral reformers with no independent basis upon which to mount their critique of the practices that they see as immoral. If there are no universal, objective or absolute principles then we can only accept the prevailing practices and standards of our communities. If the kind of relativism to which virtue ethics is subject admits this kind of objection, then it would indeed be true that virtue ethics fails to fulfil two of the primary tasks of moral theory: to tell us what we morally should do and explain the obligatoriness of our moral norms.

But does virtue ethics need to succumb to this objection? Are our intuitions and assumptions immune to critique or review simply because they are socially constructed through our traditions? No individual is constrained to think just how they are taught to think and no community holds beliefs that are the exact continuations of its traditions. Community traditions are neither unified nor hegemonic. Because individuals have to make decisions in particular circumstances there is always a spark of creativity from which critique can arise. The source of such critique will be other intuitions and insights that are gained against the background of ways of life that intersect with those of the community in question. In this way, for example, in a time when slavery was widely accepted as an unfortunate but unavoidable requirement for economic prosperity, the first inklings of critique came from individuals in certain Christian churches, whose upbringing in virtue had left them with a barely articulate feeling that this practice was wrong. The Anglican clergyman Thomas Clarkson was led by a strong impression of the evils of slavery to begin, along with a group of Quakers, a campaign to abolish the slave trade. Their feeling that the practice was wrong and their decision to oppose it arose from their characters as shaped by their unconventional formation in their churches. Hearing eye-witness accounts from slave traders moved them emotionally to sympathy and concern, and their understanding of the economic exploitation of the slaves' work led them to righteous indignation at the injustice involved in slavery. Their practical reason was exercised with a view to forming a viable course of action in the light of these conflicting emotions and understandings, and their political campaigns to press for reform used rhetoric to appeal to emotion as much as to reason. It was out of the contingent and historical setting of these Christian communities that the critique of slavery arose rather than from purely theoretical and metaphysical beliefs enunciated by theorists outside any pre-existing cultural and moral context. One cannot step outside the hermeneutic circle in order to establish a moral view from nowhere, but one can critique the dominant values and standards of one's community from the creative and sensitive insights that arise from one's character as shaped in specific communities.

My argument is that the objection to the relativism of virtue ethics on the grounds that it would not permit rational critique of immoral practices fails on two grounds. First there is no uncontentious, objective, metaphysical or *a priori* foundation from which to mount such a critique. And secondly, character as shaped by community or tradition can motivate such a critique because of its inherent creativity and sensitivity to value.

Moral psychology

I mentioned in the introduction that moral theories are either based upon, or imply, theories of human nature or a "moral psychology". Kant's moral theory, for example, implies that the human person has discrete faculties such as "reason" and "inclination" and then insists that moral decisions should be taken on the basis of reason alone. Kant insisted that the only feature of human beings that had moral worth was their will, which was conceived as the faculty of their rational decision-making. Even to act from love was not morally worthy since love was a sentiment that reduced our ability to think clearly. This form of dualism, which posits a distinction between reason and non-rational motivators such as emotion, desire and inclination, is characteristic of most duty-centred moral theories from Plato to today. Even today, most people interpret the moral struggle that they sometimes undergo in difficult situations as a struggle between reason and base inclinations. This is why most theories of duty put such a stress on reason and see it as the task of reason to control and channel the desires that arise in less worthy parts of our being.

Moreover, this reason–desire dualism maps onto the classical soul–body and Cartesian mind–body distinctions. Reason is said to be a feature of the soul or of the mind in its pure form whereas emotions are said to arise from the body and from our biological natures. Moral goodness was seen as a quality of the soul, whereas the body was the source of distraction and temptation. This even led some theorists to suggest that women were not capable of being moral since their motivations were dominated by their bodies, feelings and emotions.

This is not the place to debate these very large philosophical issues, but it is worth noting that virtue ethics thinks of the human agent in more holistic terms. In so far as well-ingrained virtues are habits acquired through instruction and practice, they are inscribed into the body. Just as trained musicians will have their skills incorporated into their very hands – it is of no use to think about a sonata and imagine its beauty if your fingers are not able to play it – so a person of good character will directly and viscerally respond to situations that call for ethical concern. As soon as a generous person sees another in need, they will feel an inclination in their bodies to help as well as being moved to think about what they might do. I have already stressed the importance of emotions in a person of virtue. It is because they care about others that kindly people will be moved to help and this caring will be felt in the body as distress at the suffering of others and joy at its relief, along with the feelings of being motivated to engage in practical deliberation.

A further analogy to explicate this point arises from sport. Although it is not central to the sphere of morality as conceived by duty ethics, sport illustrates the nature of virtue very well. It involves characteristics that people admire: characteristics such as skill, speed, tenacity, courage, team-work, determination and a preparedness to sacrifice pleasure while training for the sake of achievement. Many of these admirable traits are virtues that can also be displayed in other fields of endeavour. But the key point I want to make at this juncture is that these qualities are inscribed into and displayed in the bodies of the sportsmen and sportswomen whom we admire. It is their fitness and their skill in playing the game and in competing that displays these virtues. They are not just mental qualities and, in particular, they are not purely qualities of reason or of thinking. Although they are present in their mindsets and attitudes, the pre-eminent locus of these qualities is in the bodies of the athletes and in the way they play the game. In this way, as a specific sphere of virtue, sport illustrates the celebration of the body that the holism of virtue ethics permits.

II

In stressing practical reason to the exclusion of other motivators, duty ethics shares with the mainstream philosophical tradition of the West a considerable faith in the lucidity of consciousness. Ever since Socrates said "Know thyself" it has been assumed that reflection gives us privileged access into our own thinking. Descartes encouraged this tradition of thought with his conception of a mind that was like a theatre stage upon which the input of perception and thought played itself out before the "eye of the mind" engaged in introspection. Clear-headed people, it is assumed, can know themselves and understand their own motivations and purposes. Such persons can also think impartially and know that they are being impartial. They can think logically and know that they are being logical. And, with suitable self-control, they can deliberate without any distractions from desires or inclinations that may be lurking in the darker recesses of their minds. The notion of practical reason that is central to duty ethics assumes this conception of the human person. Unless such assumptions were made, it was argued, agents could not be held responsible for their actions. Unless the motivators to action were lucid to the agents themselves we would have to think of them as in the grip of inclinations, emotions, or desires of which they had no knowledge. And if they had no knowledge of them, then they could not be responsible for them either since they could not have controlled them. It would follow that their actions would be as involuntary as the impulsive actions of the drunk or the insane.

Ever since Sigmund Freud we have not been as confident as this about the lucidity of consciousness. We now know that we can be moved by motivators – whether they be described as "drives" or "instincts" – of which we are not aware or of which we can only become aware after considerable effort. Moreover, philosophers have questioned the Cartesian conception of a mind transparent to its own introspection. It follows that it can no longer be maintained that the first step towards being moral is to think rationally and self-consciously in a way that we can know is abstracted from our internal and hidden motivators. Instead, the first step to being moral is to be trained to act well and to thereby internalize the motivators that lead us to act well. This can be a process of which the agent is not fully aware. It is enough that the parents and teachers of this budding moral agent have some idea of what they are doing. When young persons come to know themselves and their world in their own limited terms, they will find that they have ethical attitudes, moral convictions and interpersonal attachments already in place and their practical thinking will be situated within a pre-formed motivational field of which they are barely aware. The stress that virtue ethics places upon character acknowledges the relative lack of self-knowledge that is typical of the human condition. As good literature and cinema illustrate, we often do not understand our own motivations. It follows that you cannot know whether your moral deliberation is entirely free of bias or whether your ethical stance is fully impartial. (To be fair to him, even Kant admitted that we can never be sure that we have acted from the motive of duty.) You can only hope that the inclinations and prejudices that have been developed in you as part of your upbringing will have been ethical ones. If you come to think that they are not – and this thought will initially arise from a visceral feeling of disquiet at the ethical commitments that seem to come naturally to you – then you will have to engage in considerable effort to change yourself for the better. We never fully know ourselves and we never fully control ourselves from a position of pure and self-aware reason.

III

Another deeply ingrained assumption of duty ethics is that moral agents are individuals conceived as "social atoms". What I mean by this is that the individual moral agent is seen as deciding what to do in a pure and abstract way without reference to any emotional attachments that they might have. The notion of a "social atom" captures this because in classical physics an atom is a self-enclosed and self-sufficient entity that can enter into interactions with other atoms only by impacting on them or being impacted upon by them externally. There is no internal link between atoms: no bonds of affection or ties of community. This is best illustrated by the story of the burning building that contains the brilliant scientist and your aged mother. Impartialist thinking demands that you save the person who could bring the greatest benefit to others. You are urged to disregard your attachment to your mother. Given that your attachment to your mother gives rise to an inclination or emotion that should not be allowed to influence your moral decision-making, such attachments should be disregarded. Duty ethics often envisages the ideal moral agent as an individual unencumbered by the kinds of attachment that would distract decision-making from what duty demands.

The discourse of rights, duties and obligations is a discourse that seeks to create connections between persons conceived as social atoms based on external reasons arising from moral theory. Many moral theorists explicate such connections using the model of a contract. I am obliged to you to provide a bag of potatoes and you have a right to claim the potatoes from me if we have entered into a contract by your paying me for those potatoes. Not all contracts are explicit and written on a piece of paper and the "social contract" that is posited by moral theorists to establish civil society as a mutual system of obligations and rights is an implicit contract in this way. As a result of such a contract, the only bond that I have with you in the world of duty ethics is the obligation that I have towards you or the right that you can claim against me that pure and impartial thought will have established theoretically. Any other physical or affective bond must be ignored.

In contrast, virtue ethics conceives of human beings as interdependent and social in their very being. We are not first discrete entities that then enter into quasi-contractual arrangements. We are brought up within family and community bonds. Virtue ethics recognizes that we do not enter the sphere of morality as fully formed autonomous individuals. We are first of all children. As children we live a life of dependency upon our parents or others who fill the role of parents. We are needy and we form bonds of dependency and affection with those who fill our needs. Our parents and teachers provide not only nurture and sustenance but also the formation of our characters. They teach us how to behave, what exemplars of virtuous behaviour to emulate, what ways of life to admire and what things of value to respect and respond to. In so far as these lessons are taught within the context of nurturing and caring relationships they are invested with a sense of importance. Our love for our nurturers becomes expressible in the way in which we adhere to the norms and ideals that they have taught us. We become inclined to do the virtuous thing even before we rationally evaluate why it is virtuous. This inclination is a motivator that precedes the development of our rational powers and that can never be completely superseded by those powers, although we may come to feel that those inclinations should be critiqued and reshaped. To insist that we must approach moral decision-making with *a priori* reason is to ignore the way in which we develop as human beings.

The nature of moral judgements about others

I

Part of the task of moral theory is to explain and justify not only our own moral decisions but also our moral judgements about others. The judgements made by the ethics of duty are "agent-neutral", whereas the judgements made by virtue ethics are agent-relative. Duty ethics would insist that if an action is right for one person, it would be right for any person in the same circumstances. All other things being equal, to return a borrowed book is an obligation for anyone who borrows a book. That moral demands are agent-neutral in this way is entirely appropriate. It is in the nature of moral duties to be general in their applicability. However, the virtue judgements we make about individuals and their actions need not be agent-neutral in this way. We may say of Mary that she is courageous in a particular situation while we do not say that Mitsuko is courageous even though she has done a similar thing in a similar situation. We know Mary to be a very shy and insecure person whereas Mitsuko always shows a lot of bravado. Accordingly, it took courage for Mary to act as she did whereas it did not require courage from Mitsuko. So the judgement that Mary is courageous is "agent-relative" because it is made in the light of what we know of Mary's character and of how she made her decision.

II

A supererogatory act is an act that is good to perform but is not required by duty. To help someone when there are plenty of other people around who are willing to help would be an example. Another example would be to study hard for a test that you are already sure of passing. Such actions fall outside the scope of duty and need to be understood in terms of such thick concepts of human virtue as "generosity" or "diligence". Accordingly, the notion of "supererogatory action" operates differently in the two traditions of ethical theory.

The main reason for this difference is that the notion of "good" operates differently in the two traditions. Indeed, as I indicated in "Moral terminology" §IV, in the ethics of duty it is largely replaced by the more juridical notion of "right". It is of primary importance to do the right thing and to avoid doing the wrong thing. To be a good person is simply to be innocent of any wrongdoing. Although it may also be possible to be good by doing things that are above and beyond the call of duty – that is, to perform supererogatory actions – the central issue is to do the right thing. Virtue ethicists, on the other hand, recognize that people admire one another for a great variety of good qualities. We admire courage, tolerance, reverence, integrity, humility, justified pride, fortitude and a whole host of positive traits of character. We dislike and even despise dishonesty, deviousness, obsequiousness, vanity, laziness and a whole host of vices. And our feelings of approval or disapproval admit many degrees of intensity. As opposed to the either/or of good/evil or right/wrong judgements, our virtue evaluations are qualitative along several axes. There will be our understanding of the situation and hence of what virtue is being displayed. There will be our evaluation of the importance of what is ethically salient in the situation. There will also be our understanding of the person and of their personal history so that we appreciate how easy or difficult it is for them to act virtuously. In short, the judgements of others that we make from a virtue perspective are complex, multi-levelled and sensitive. Like the decisions we make from this perspective, they are particular to specific situations rather than general in form. And we are as prone to praise people who display virtue as to impose shame on those who fail to. People can be good in many ways and not all of these will relate to specific duties. Accordingly, virtue ethics will see many good actions as supererogatory but it will not see this as a problem. Actions above and beyond the call of duty are just what you would expect from good and virtuous people.

Summary and conclusion

This chapter has detailed twenty-three contrasts between an ethics of duty and virtue ethics. The best way to summarize them is to refer back to Table 1. However, my intention was not just to display a series of differences between the two traditions. It was also to suggest the following:

- Virtue ethics does a better job at performing the four tasks of moral theory: to understand morality, to prescribe norms, to justify them and to describe how they fit into our lives.
- It understands morality as a social construct that has the function of ordering social life and giving meaning to the lives of individuals.
- It prescribes norms in that it stipulates what traits of character and what characteristic behaviours are admirable and it justifies these norms by showing how those traits and behaviours are conducive to an ordered social life and a meaningful personal existence.
- Most importantly, virtue ethics gives a description of our social lives and depends upon a philosophical conception of human existence that is true to life.
- These suggestions have tended to challenge some of the central doctrines of the tradition of duty ethics: those of moral realism and the objectivity of moral norms, of the centrality of reason in our lives and of the concept of right action.

But this chapter has not been able to argue for any of these suggestions in any detail. Indeed, it is not within the scope of this book to pursue the critique of the various forms of duty ethics any further. What I propose to do in the chapters that follow is to provide a deeper theoretical grounding for the remarks that I have made about virtue ethics and also to show that some of the central tasks of moral theory can be fulfilled by it. Accordingly, I turn in the next chapter to the ideas of Aristotle, whose theory I rely upon in broad terms in order to justify my own position. Through this discussion I shall show particularly that virtue ethics is more true to our understanding of ourselves as moral agents than the ethics of duty.

two

Aristotle's ethics

The aims of life

In this chapter I shall conduct a quick tour of a central work by Aristotle (384–323 BCE): *Nicomachean Ethics*. This book is not primarily about morality as we understand it today. What Aristotle means by "ethics" may be discerned if we consider the ancient Greek root of the term: *ethos*. This term refers to the customs of a society, including the characteristic outlook on life that is held by most members of that society. To speak about ethics in this sense is to speak about the customary behaviour of a people, the standards of human excellence they hold themselves bound to, and the attitudes through which they express their character as a people. These will include the attitudes that they have to one another. What kind of person do people in a particular society admire? What kinds of actions do they praise and what kinds of actions do they despise? Further, Aristotle is offering us a theory about human beings and what it is for them to flourish: a theory that will ground sound advice on how to live life well. He does not take himself to be laying down the moral law for his fellow citizens of ancient Athens. He takes it for granted that everyone understands what actions are wrong and that no one would be tempted to think that murdering someone, for example, could be any part of an answer to the question of how we should live our lives. What we would think of today as moral prohibitions of this kind were not up for discussion in Aristotle's text because attitudes towards them were not optional and were not a matter for individual judgement. For Aristotle the issue was "How should we live well?" rather than "What is the morally right thing to do?"

> If then, our activities have some end which we want for its own sake, and for the sake of which we want all the other ends – if we do not choose everything for the sake of something else (for this will involve an infinite progression, so that our aim will be pointless and ineffectual) – it is clear that this must be the Good, that is the supreme good.
>
> Aristotle, *Nicomachean Ethics*, 1094a17–22

Aristotle begins his book by saying that the good or goal towards which we aim in any given project can itself be questioned as to what it is good for. If I say that I am studying philosophy in order to increase my job prospects, I can go on to ask why I would want to increase my job prospects. And if I answer by saying that I want more money I can then go on to ask why I want more money. And if I say it is because I want to live in luxury I can ask why I want to live in luxury, and so on. At some point I am likely to reach an answer such as "Because I want to be happy", and this is a point beyond which my questioning cannot go. Why not? Because it does not make any sense to ask "Why do I want to be happy?" This is a goal or a good that does not need any further reason or justification. The series of questions "Why is that a good or a worthwhile goal?" comes to an end when you have identified a goal that justifies itself or needs no further justification. Aristotle claims that there is one end-point for any such series of questions: one thing that we all want for its own sake. And he calls this "the Good".

Aristotle explains that the Good for human beings consists in *eudaimoniā* (a Greek word combining *eu* meaning "good" with *daimon* meaning "spirit", and most often translated as "happiness"). Whereas he had argued in a purely formal way that the Good was that to which we all aim, he now gives a more substantive answer: that this universal human goal is happiness. However, he is quick to point out that this conclusion is still somewhat formal since different people have different views about what happiness is. Some people say it is worldly enjoyment while others say it is eternal salvation. Aristotle's theory will turn out to be "naturalistic" in that it does not depend on any theological or metaphysical knowledge. It does not depend on knowledge of God or of metaphysical and universal moral norms. It depends only on knowledge of human nature and other worldly and social realities. For him it is the study of human nature and worldly existence that will disclose the relevant meaning of the notion of *eudaimoniā*.

Aristotle's thinking is teleological (from the Greek words, *telos* meaning "goal" and *logos* meaning "knowledge"). This means that he understands things in terms of the goals that they pursue and the functions that they are designed to perform. Note that a "goal" in this sense does not need to be a purpose that is consciously entertained by the thing that is said to have the goal. Just as a plant evinces the goal of growing and propagating itself (witness the striving of a weed that forces its way through the concrete of a car park), and an animal evinces the goal of surviving long enough to propagate itself into the next generation, so human beings also evince goals. Aristotle takes the example of a flautist. The goal, purpose or function of a flautist is to play the flute and to do so as well as possible. In a similar way, suggests Aristotle, human beings have a goal or a function. In a purely schematic way we might say that the goal of a human existence is to do those things that are distinctly human and to do them well: that is, to be good *as a human being*. Now the activities that are distinctly human are rational activities since Aristotle thinks that a human being is an animal that is distinguished from other animals in being rational. So the fulfilment of the functions of a human being, or being good at being a human being, consists in the exercise of rationality in actions that are rational. Aristotle refers to the rational activity that will make us happy as virtuous activity. We shall be happy, he says, when we act in accordance with virtue and we shall be most happy when we act in accordance with the highest form of virtue. This teleological schema provides the basic structure of Aristotle's book.

Accordingly, any discussion of ethics, in so far as it concerns the nature and goals of human life, must discuss what it is to be a human being and what it is to fulfil the tendencies inherent in our nature as human beings. Aristotle gives us his conception of what a human being is by describing the human soul. He identified four "parts of the soul" as making up a full human being. These were the vegetative, the appetitive, the deliberative and the contemplative. Because these categories are so important I shall spend some time describing them and anticipating some of the ways in which Aristotle will make use of them later in the text.

The vegetative level

The vegetative level of our existence is what we would describe today as the biological functioning of our bodies. It consists in those many processes of growth, metabolism, blood circulation and so forth that make up the dynamic operation of our bodily existence. The vegetative aspect of our being is the body conceived as a machine. Do note, however, that while the body as machine was conceived by Cartesian modernism as an objectified and purely biological entity – a body without personality or subjectivity – Aristotle does not theorize the body in this abstracted way. His premodern terminology of "parts of the soul" makes it clear that he is talking about an aspect of a whole. The soul is the whole, single and distinctive animating principle of the person and to delineate a "part" of it is not to identify an entity that constitutes a portion of a larger whole in the way that an engine is a part of a car: the part that makes it move. Rather, we should think of Aristotle as identifying different kinds of functioning that make up the whole living, active and thoughtful person. The vegetative "part of the soul", or the living body, comprises those aspects of the dynamic existence of the human person that centrally involve her body. These aspects cannot be distinguished clearly or definitively from other aspects of human existence.

Aristotle understands the vegetative part of the soul as a mode of functioning of the person that aims at a specific goal. For him, all of the parts of the soul have a tendency or internal goal that is distinctive of them and that they seek to fulfil. I do not *use* my skin to protect me from infections and other hurts; the skin has this purpose and goal within itself. This is its internal goal and it is good *as skin* to the extent that it fulfils this goal.

The appetitive level

Aristotle's positing of an "appetitive part of the soul" is based on the obvious fact that human beings desire things and strive to attain them. Just as we share the vegetative part of our souls with plants, so we share the appetitive part of our souls with animals. It is clear just from observing them that animals desire things. Indeed, one might say that their whole lives are ruled by desires. When our pet cat is not asleep, it is constantly active in pursuit of a variety of desires that it seems to have. And this also applies to human beings.

That we have appetites and desires is undeniable. It is in the nature of the kind of being that we are to be desirous, to be directed upon things that we want and a future that we seek, and to be striving for the objects of our inclination. We are not just passive beings to whom things happen and who can only act if caused to do so by external forces. Our desires and motivations are the internal sources of the energy and enthusiasm with which we approach life.

The appetitive aspect of our being also allows us to understand emotion and feeling. In so far as desire generates movement in our being towards cognition, action and reaction, there is a dynamic aspect of our existence the flow of which is often experienced as feeling. Not only are we actively engaged with the world and with others but we experience that engagement as desire, curiosity, longing and enjoyment. When desire is frustrated we feel pain or anguish. When such feelings are integrated with cognition we experience emotions. Such emotions as fear, anger or joy combine a cognitive grasp of the situation in which we find ourselves with inchoate feelings. Were we not desiring beings, such reactions would not occur in us. And nor would they were we not whole and integrated beings. The cognitive dimension of existence needs to be present for emotion to be possible. Even an animal needs to apprehend the danger in its environment in some way in order to express its tendency towards survival by feeling fear and taking flight.

Notice that the desiring aspect of our being is also fundamentally teleological. Indeed, it is almost definitive of what teleology means for Aristotle. To be desirous of something is the human or animal way of having a tendency towards a goal. Whether or not the desire is present to consciousness, it constitutes the orientation of the organism towards that which would meet its need or fulfil its tendency. But these would be external goals of the organism. The internal goal of desire or appetite might be understood, not as a desire for something outside the organism, such as a child's desire for ice cream, but as a comportment of the organism towards its own fulfilment. In order to distinguish this idea from the common-sense notion of desire where desire is always a desire for some object, Aristotle suggests that the appetitive aspect of our being is the tendency of the organism to seek its own fulfilment through the excellence of its desires. This fulfilment is not only the excellent pursuit of its desires or the successful attainment of its desires, but also the having of desires that perfect its being. Desiring the right things is as important as obtaining what is desired. In this way a person who desires drugs of addiction would not fulfil the internal goal of her being whether or not she obtains what she desires. This is a self-destructive desire to have.

As we shall see later, it is this point that allows Aristotle to draw the ethical implication that we should desire well, and he understands this not only in terms of the external objects of our desire, but also in terms of such internal qualities as the intensity of the desire and whether the desire enhances our being. Our desires should be an expression of self-fulfilling inclinations and we should not be excessive or deficient in our desires. In a less moralistic tone, we might draw the conclusion that our having desires is part of what constitutes the richness and excitement of our lives. We can enjoy desiring.

The deliberative level

Aristotle distinguishes the vegetative and appetitive parts of the soul from the rational part. He thinks of this latter aspect of our being as distinctive of us as human beings and says that animals do not share in it. He then goes on to suggest that the ethical problem that all people face is that of having the rational part of their soul remain in control of the desiring part. On this view we will live our lives well if our reason controls our inclinations. This is a view that was developed by Plato and that has since been taken up by Christianity and by Kant as a description of our moral psychology. However, it will turn out that Aristotle's view of the internal psychology of human beings is considerably more complex than this. First, the rational part of the soul is itself divided into two different kinds of function – the "deliberative" and the "contemplative" – and secondly, the way in which we exercise self-control will turn out to be much more subtle than would be suggested by Plato's model.

The third part of the soul that Aristotle identifies is the "deliberative" or "calculative" part. He has in mind our ability to think about what we do, to plan our actions, to be strategic in our approach to our needs and to review the effectiveness of what we have done. Rather than being driven by instincts or habits, human beings can be rational and reflective in their approach to the exigencies of life. It is this aspect of our being that tempts modern philosophers to dualistic ways of thinking. It is this aspect of our being that leads us to posit a "faculty" called "reason" or a "thinking substance" called "mind". Aristotle makes no such mistake. He sees it as just as much an aspect or level of our whole being as the vegetative and appetitive aspects. Deliberation or rational thinking is just one of the functions that whole human beings perform and through which they can fulfil themselves in their being.

Notice that the deliberative function is also teleological in the two ways that I have identified: having internal and external goals. Our deliberation, as Aristotle will say later, is about the means that we need to attain our goals. It is strategic. In this sense it is directed to a goal. But it is also teleological in the sense that our doing it well constitutes a fulfilment of our being. In so far as we are rational beings, we enjoy exercising our intellects. That we play chess and other mind games shows that we gain a satisfaction from the sheer exercise of our deliberative functions whether or not it is directed to some purpose external to us. This internal fulfilment is the inherent goal of the deliberative aspect of our being.

The deliberative part of our being is inextricably linked to action. For Aristotle, it is distinctive of human beings that we act rationally. We engage in actions and practices that have goals, and our deliberation is our thinking about how those practical goals can be achieved. Now these goals are, once again, of two kinds. There are the more obvious external goals that are the ends that we pursue in our actions, and there are the internal goals, which are the satisfactions that come from doing the job well. They are internal in the sense that the agent experiences them, more or less self-consciously, as feelings of attainment, or of enjoyment in the exercise of the task. Just as a craftsman relishing the sheer physical activity of working with his materials would be an example of the fulfil-ment of the appetitive aspects of his being in that his enjoyment arises from feeling himself able to overcome difficulties and from enjoying a form of physical well-being in rapport with his materials, so a worker whose job involves thinking, calculating and planning enjoys overcom-ing the difficulties that intellectual problems pose. Being rational beings, we fulfil ourselves when we think clearly, coherently and effectively so as to increase our ability to attain our goals. These rational skills are the internal goals or "excellences" of our functioning as deliberative beings in the practical spheres of life.

The contemplative level

The fourth part of the soul or aspect of our being that Aristotle iden-tifies is what he calls the contemplative part. He sees contemplation as a further aspect of our reasoning, but it is distinguished from the deliberative part in terms of what it is about: that is, in terms of its objects. Whereas deliberative reason is about the means that we need to achieve our goals and about the things we can change in the world by our actions, contemplative reason is about the things we cannot change. What Aristotle has in mind here includes the goals and values that we strive after (which he takes to be given by our human nature), the laws of physical nature that order the way the world works, and the nature and will of the gods. In brief, Aristotle suggests that the contemplative aspect of our being is detached from our active lives and is fulfilled by thinking about eternal and changeless things. Examples of such think-ing would include theoretical physics, mathematics, philosophy and theology. I think of it as a form of theoretical thinking that has as its goal the understanding of the universe and of our existence in it, and that has as its internal satisfaction and fulfilment the creation of a sense of wholeness and meaningfulness in our lives. We are interested in such big questions as the origin and nature of the universe, the source and meaning of morality, the existence or non-existence of God and the significance of beauty and truth in our lives, because thinking about such things (whether or not we achieve answers) is part of what makes our lives meaningful. Moreover, having a theory about such things (whether we acquire it from our cultures or by our own efforts) gives our lives an integrity or structure in which day-to-day events can gain their meaning as part of a coherent whole. It allows us to feel that we are part of a larger story or reality.

The fulfilment of this aspect of our being does not necessarily consist in gaining demonstrably true answers to our theoretical questions. Rather, the fulfilment of this aspect of our being consists in contemplating well. This means being honest with ourselves and being consistent. It means not clinging to false hopes or merely comforting theories if they are inconsistent with our other beliefs. It means having faith that is not superstition. It means not being superficial or shallow. And it means being able to affirm life with our most spiritual intellect as well as our deepest emotion.

Virtues of character

As we have just seen, Aristotle distinguished the vegetative and appetitive functions of the soul from the rational functions (which he later divides into calculative and contemplative). In so far as he chooses to disregard the vegetative part of the soul further, we can summarize Aristotle's distinction as being a twofold distinction between the desiring functions and the rational functions. Each of these kinds of function can be exercised well or poorly. When we exercise them well we display virtue. Accordingly, there are two kinds of virtue, corresponding to the two kinds of function. There are the "intellectual" virtues that consist in exercising our rational functions well, and there are the virtues of character (often translated misleadingly as "the moral virtues") that consist in exercising our appetitive functions well. In this section we shall explore the virtues of character.

The intellectual virtues are the result of teaching and the virtues of character are the result of the training of habit. We are not born virtuous. This is interesting because it is arguable that we are born with certain character traits and talents. Some children seem "naturally" more boisterous than others and some seem more tentative from an early age. While theorists debate the issue of "nature or nurture" at great length, it does seem that some basic patterns of personality are genetic. It is certainly clear that our talents are. That some people's fingers move more easily over the piano keyboard, or that some people are tall and agile enough to be good at basketball seems to be a product of natural endowment. This is not to deny that practice and training can make up for a lack of natural advantage in some cases, but there are other cases where natural talent clearly contributes to the accomplishments that a person displays in life. However, these natural abilities are not deemed to be virtues, even though they are admirable and may contribute to *eudaimoniā*. Even if being a good piano player requires that we have some talent, it is also obvious that it requires practice. It is much the same with virtue, says Aristotle. Although we are not born with virtue, nature does give us the basic ability to be virtuous. But we need to practise virtue in order to acquire it. We need to get into the habit of acting virtuously and this habit will then become a disposition to act in that way. We acquire, for example, the virtue of courage by doing courageous things. We should avoid being either foolhardy or cowardly. If we act in either of these ways, we shall acquire the habit of acting in that way and we shall not acquire the virtue of courage, whereas if we face up to danger bravely on a number of occasions, we shall gradually become courageous.

But if we become virtuous by performing virtuous actions, how can we start to become virtuous? What would lead us to that first courageous or generous action if we were not already virtuous? Aristotle's answer to this is that others have to train us. We must be rewarded for doing the virtuous thing and punished for doing the vicious thing. In this way we shall acquire the habit without, at first, knowing what the virtue is and without having the disposition to act virtuously. The first steps towards virtue are the result of encouragement and training.

How would I know whether my training in virtue was complete? When could I know that I had become virtuous? Others might tell me by what they say or by how they come to trust me with difficult tasks, but I would also be able to tell by how I react to situations of temptation. If I react to situations of danger with the feeling that I want to run away and hide then I am not courageous, whereas if I face the situation without distress, I am. Aristotle's subsequent discussion of courage makes it clear that he does not suggest that being courageous implies not feeling any fear. It is quite appropriate to feel fear in the face of danger. To not do so would be to misunderstand the situation that one was in or to be insensitive to what was important in it. It is how we handle fear that defines us as courageous. If it leads us to want to run then our disposition is not courageous, whereas if we feel ourselves willing and able to face our fear, then that shows that we have acquired the habit or disposition to be courageous. Similarly, a person who wants to give money to the needy and positively enjoys doing so is truly generous. If you have to force yourself to give to a cause that you judge to be worthy, then you are having to fight against inclinations that show that you are not yet a generous person. A generous person would not feel the inclination to be stingy and a courageous person would not feel the inclination to run from danger. Accordingly, to be virtuous is more than acquiring a habit or a disposition to act in a certain way. It involves wanting to act in that way.

> But virtuous acts are not done in a just or temperate way merely because *they* have a certain quality, but only if the agent also acts in a certain state, viz. (1) if he knows what he is doing, (2) if he chooses it, and chooses it for its own sake, and (3) if he does it from a fixed and permanent disposition.
> Aristotle, *Nicomachean Ethics*, 1105a28–34

Aristotle argues that if virtue consisted only in trained behaviour then it would seem to be enough for an action to look virtuous for it to be virtuous. It would only be the outward behaviour that mattered. A youth being trained to be generous could give alms to the needy and thereby look virtuous and could even have acquired the habit of doing so. But is this enough to make him virtuous? No, as Aristotle has already said, he must also enjoy doing so if we are to regard him as truly virtuous. There is an important internal dimension to virtue. Not only must the virtuous person be glad to be acting virtuously, but he must also know what he is doing, choose to do it for its own sake (not for the sake of the praise that one might receive or for the sake of forming the habit of acting virtuously), and have the disposition of character to act in that way. So he is only truly virtuous when he has internalized the habit, along with the relevant attitudes and understandings, of the virtue into which he has been trained.

Aristotle defines virtue as a disposition rather than a feeling or a faculty. He has already argued for this by saying that it is acquired by habit and that we are not born with it (as we are with our faculties), and by saying just how feelings are involved (namely, as an indication that one has acquired a virtue). Aristotle then goes on to say how a virtuous disposition differs from other dispositions. A virtue is a disposition that makes us good as a human being in that it makes us perform our functions well. Given our teleological nature, what is good for us is that we fulfil the tendencies and goals of our natures. Accordingly, any state or action that consists in our fulfilling our functions well is a virtue. In the case of the virtues of character that are concerned with the appetitive parts of the soul, this means that desiring well is what virtue consists in.

> So too it is easy to get angry – anyone can do that – or to give and spend money; but to feel or act towards the right person to the right extent at the right time for the right reason in the right way – that is not easy, and it is not everyone that can do it. Hence to do these things well is a rare, laudable, and fine achievement. Aristotle, *Nicomachean Ethics*, 1109a26–29

Aristotle goes on to describe a number of virtues (I list them in Chapter 5) and to give us a rule of thumb for recognizing them. In order to prepare the ground for doing this he tells us what he means by the term "the mean". He says that in some matters "the mean" simply means the average or the middle. So the mean of two and ten is six. But when we speak of "the mean relative to us" we have a different concept in mind. It is the concept of the right amount or degree: the amount or degree that avoids deficiency or excess. The word "right" here does not mean "morally correct". It means "appropriate" or "in accordance with the mean for that person". To act virtuously in a specific situation is to avoid the deficiencies or excesses that that situation presents to the agent as temptations or problems to be avoided. Courage, for example, is the mean between cowardliness and foolhardiness. Aristotle makes the point that what is right or appropriate cannot be worked out in abstract or quasi-mathematical terms. It has to be judged in relation to the particular individual involved. A suitable meal for a supermodel would be different from a suitable meal for a Sumo wrestler.

Many people have interpreted Aristotle to be saying that, to be virtuous, a person should always act in a moderate way. This would be the view that virtue consists in avoiding extremes and taking a measured approach to life. They then criticize this view on the grounds that it seems to applaud mediocrity. On this view the sorts of commitment and determination that make for artistic achievement, sports heroism, loyalty under pressure and military courage would be ruled out on the grounds of being excessive. And there are certainly many passages in which this is what Aristotle seems to be saying. However, I would argue that Aristotle does not mean this. The "mean" is relative to the person acting and to the situation she is in. Some situations do call for highly intense responses. Great danger calls for high courage. Great challenges call for extreme effort and so on. Acting "rightly" in such situations would indeed go beyond the mediocre or moderate response. Aristotle is not preaching moderation in all things. But he is talking about the habits and disposition that we should have and it would make no sense to say that we should be in the habit of acting in an extreme way. By their very nature extreme or intense actions would not be habitual. They would not be what we are normally disposed to do. Occasionally, situations will call for heroic responses but our normal dispositions are attuned to the everyday rather than to the unusual.

In unusual or extreme situations a person will have to exercise judgement and, in so far as this involves the intellectual virtues, Aristotle is not yet ready to discuss what this amounts to. In so far as he is discussing the virtues of character by themselves at the moment, he can only be talking about relatively routine situations in which we act in accordance with our habits and dispositions. In such situations we do not give much thought to what we do and do not exercise our judgement. In so far as we are acting from our dispositions, therefore, it would be best if our dispositions were to act in accordance with the mean: that is, in such a way as to avoid excess or deficiency. It is only in extreme situations that we need to exercise judgement and see what unusual and intense actions are required of us. So Aristotle is not advocating mediocrity or moderation in all things. He is just saying that in everyday life, when we do not have to think about what we are doing, we had best have a disposition to do what is the mean for us in that situation.

> So virtue is a purposive disposition, lying in a mean that is relative to us and determined by a rational principle, and by that which a prudent man would use to determine it. It is a mean between two kinds of vice, one of excess and the other of deficiency.
>
> Aristotle, *Nicomachean Ethics*, 1106b36–1107a3

Aristotle's definition of virtue merits close study. Aristotle begins by calling virtue a "purposive disposition". This means that it is a disposition to perform purposive actions. In more modern terms we might say that it relates to actions that we perform intentionally or "on purpose". He then says that the disposition is a disposition to actions that lie in a mean that is relative to us and determined by a rational principle. We have already seen what this means. The actions that a virtuous person is disposed to perform are those that avoid extremes where what this means in a particular concrete case is specified relative to the circumstances of the person involved and, moreover, determined by a judgement of what the appropriate or "mean" course of action would be. Aristotle refers to a "rational principle" because he expects that the judgement made as to what the mean or appropriate course of action would be in a given situation will be determined by a judgement that is rational and well informed. How those judgements should be made is a matter that he will discuss when he turns to the intellectual virtues in Book 6 of his text. At this point he says nothing more than that the rational principle involved would be that which a prudent man would use. Since he has not yet explained to us what prudence is, he cannot spell this out any more fully at this point. His intention here is simply to suggest that if you do not have the necessary intellectual skills or virtues to make the judgement as to what the appropriate action would be in a given situation, and if you do not have a habit to act in the appropriate way in such situations, then you had better take the advice of a prudent person and act in the way that he or she would.

Aristotle's doctrine of the virtues of character as the mean is not his final and considered position. The fully virtuous person certainly has dispositions to avoid extremes, but he also has the discernment to see what a given situation calls for. The younger person who is not yet fully formed in all the virtues and is still struggling to acquire the virtues of character can only depend on the notion of virtue as a mean and on rules of thumb for finding what that mean is. This is laudable, but it is not mature virtue. Aristotle's doctrine of virtue as the mean is only a part of a fuller picture of virtue that he is developing. What is needed further is judgement.

Pleasure as an ethical problem

Before moving on to the question of what judgement is and to the more general topic of what the intellectual virtues are, we should discuss at least one of the virtues of character that Aristotle analyses: temperance. I choose to explicate his view of temperance because it illustrates very well Aristotle's typical approach to the virtues of character, and also because it raises ethical issues that are broader than the more limited domain of morality.

The first point that Aristotle makes (1117b22) is that temperance is a virtue that belongs to the "irrational part of the soul". You will recall that this would mean the desiring or appetitive part of the soul. So this is a virtue of managing one's desires. The object of the relevant desire is pleasure and the virtue of temperance concerns itself with the proper management of the desire for pleasure. While one can be excessive or deficient in avoiding pain, the central meaning of temperance for Aristotle is that it is the mean between being too preoccupied with pleasure (licentiousness) and having too little interest in it (insensibility). For Aristotle, not being attracted to the pleasurable things of life is just as much an ethical failure as indulging in them to excess.

Aristotle goes on to say that the kinds of pleasure that cause ethical problems are those that involve physical contact with the object of pleasure. This places the focus squarely on food, drink and sex. The pleasures of connoisseurship, like those of listening to beautiful music, looking at great art or discussing noble ideas, seem not to be a problem for Aristotle. But this raises some interesting points for discussion. Is it not possible to enjoy these finer pleasures – ones that do not involve touching the object of pleasure, but merely contemplating it or listening to it – in just as problematic a way as more sensual pleasures? If someone spent all their time and money on such pursuits would this still not be excessive and therefore not virtuous? This raises the question as to why we think the excessive pursuit of pleasure is an ethical problem. If we think it is an ethical problem because it takes away time and resources from more noble or necessary pursuits, then taking an excessive interest in the arts, or in hiking, or in stamp collecting, or in food, drink and sex are all equally bad and for the same reason. We may think that people ought to spend their time and money looking after their family and meeting their other obligations and that they should pursue pleasure only after their obligations have been met. From this point of view the fault of licentiousness or of any excessive activity is that it leads one to neglect one's responsibilities in favour of pleasure and enjoyment.

But this is not Aristotle's reason for thinking of licentiousness as a vice. He is not a utilitarian: one who thinks that wrong actions are wrong because they cause unhappiness as a consequence. Aristotle does not think that all forms of self-indulgence or enjoyment have the same ethical standing or involve the same ethical danger: that of causing unhappiness to others or even to oneself. For Aristotle, the pleasures of the flesh (food, drink and sex) have a special ethical significance because they are pleasures of the body rather than of the mind. In more technical terms they are pleasures of the appetitive part of our souls rather than of the rational part of the soul. Listening to beautiful music and appreciating great art involve intellectual skills and knowledge. We might say that they are pleasures that have a spiritual dimension to them. These are pleasures that are distinctive of us as cultured and educated human beings and, as such, they ennoble us rather than degrade us. In contrast, the problem with physical pleasure is that we share it with animals and so it degrades us to indulge in it. In so far as Aristotle thinks of human beings as rational animals – creatures that are more noble than animals by virtue of being rational and having a more complex soul – we should fulfil our more noble faculties and not demean ourselves by wallowing in those pleasures that belong to our animal natures.

This point of view on pleasure has been taken up in our cultural history by many strands of thought, most notably that of the Christian religion. This tradition would suggest that, in so far as we are children of God, with an eternal and glorious destiny as disembodied beings in heaven, we should focus our lives on the more spiritual and lofty aspects of our being. The pleasures of the flesh cannot but be a distraction from this. When nineteenth-century puritans urged people to give up drink and to confine their sexual activities to the marriage bed (and then only modestly) they stood in a very ancient tradition. And when contemporary commentators and churchmen fulminate against our "materialistic" and hedonistic culture their thinking is structured by the same set of ideas. There is much to discuss here and it would be interesting to develop a philosophy of pleasure that would not lead to an attitude of puritanism.

Aristotle discusses the role of reason in relation to pleasure in the very last sentences of Book 3. The image that he gives there is one of control. It is an image that he has inherited from Plato. According to this image, the rational part of the soul should control the desiderative or appetitive part. Reason should control desire. The implication is that desire is, of its own nature, irrational and unruly. Left to its power a person would be constantly pursuing pleasure and self-indulgence and would lack any coherence or structure to their lives. They would desire anything pleasurable indiscriminately, and without inhibition or limit. Such a life would be dissolute and would lead to great harm for the self and even to self-destruction. It would be much better, then, for the rational part of the soul to control the desires and order them in accordance with rational principles.

It would do this in two ways. First, it would ensure that one did not desire things excessively (or not enough, although Aristotle no longer considers this possibility). It might be rationally acceptable to desire and take one slice of cheesecake, but to take two or more slices is excessive. Rationality would define what is the "mean" for the person involved. Secondly, reason would ensure that we desire things that are consistent with our overarching goal of happiness or *eudaimoniā*. We would be led by reason to reject the second or third slice of cheesecake not just because to take them would be excessive but because eating that much cheesecake (at least on a regular basis) is not good for our health. Given that health is constitutive of happiness and is thus a rational goal to pursue, reason would urge us to not desire things that could ruin our health. As Aristotle had put it earlier (1118b26), the licentious man goes wrong not just in "enjoying things with abnormal intensity", but also in "enjoying the wrong objects".

This image of the relation between desire and reason is a familiar one and it finds support in Aristotle's text. However, I do not consider that it is his final position on the issue. My reason for saying this is that it does not suggest a holistic picture of our psychology. Creating a model in which reason rules the appetites in this way creates a split between reason and desire. It implies that desire is a separate faculty (or part of the soul) from reason and does not participate in any way in our rationality. On this picture, desire is at best non-rational and at worst mad. But we know that our desires can be rational. We desire justice. We desire a beautiful environment. We desire good and wholesome food. We desire sex with the one we love. Are these desires not inherently rational rather than desires that are inherently mad but controlled by a separate faculty of reason? And what of our reason? When we judge something to be good, do we not also desire or enjoy it? When we judge that something is a good thing to do, does this not also motivate us to do it? When we judge a book to be well written, do we not also enjoy reading it? When we eat a fine meal, does our understanding of the cuisine not add to our enjoyment? It would seem that reason and desire, the rational part of the soul and the appetitive, are not so separate that we can speak of the one controlling the other.

Aristotle himself is not unaware of these problems. He gives a hint of this in his remarks about licentiousness being more "voluntary" than cowardice. What he means by this is that the coward is often overcome by his fear and so his action in fleeing the field of battle is not the result of choice. The coward is forced by the desiderative or appetitive part of his soul to flee, much as the passenger on the ship is forced by the storm to travel to Syracuse. The wind blows him off course. But pleasure does not force us in this way. It does not overcome us – at least typically. (There are some totally degenerate people, Aristotle says later, who are indeed the prisoners of their desires.) The licentious person *chooses* pleasure as a goal rather than having it control his life. And then Aristotle says that for the licentious man "particular acts are voluntary, since he does them from desire and appetite" (1119a31). But he had already defined a voluntary act as one arising from choice. Choice is "deliberate appetition": that is to say, appetite structured by reason. The licentious man has a policy of pursuing pleasure. While this is a policy that another more virtuous or rational person might not share, it is a policy that makes it rational for him to choose pleasure whenever the opportunity presents itself. And so he makes rational decisions on particular occasions to indulge his desires. The licentious person acts from choice. He acts voluntarily. He is not out of control and caught up in the madness of overwhelming desire. Given his policy of always choosing as much pleasure as possible, his plan for life might not be considered by temperate people as very rational. But, given his policy, his particular actions are rational because they are consistent with that policy. His choices are "deliberate appetitions". So the relation between reason and desire is not that of one controlling the other. It is a much more complex and intimate relation involving judgement, and one that we need to explore more fully.

> Thus the desiderative element of the temperate man ought to be in harmony with the rational principle; because both have the same object: the attainment of what is admirable.   Aristotle, *Nicomachean Ethics*, 1119b15–19

Wisdom and practical reason

At the beginning of Book 6, Aristotle acknowledges that his description of virtue as consisting in the avoidance of excess or deficiency does not tell us enough. We have to be able to judge what would be excessive in a particular situation and what would be deficient. If I was asked to make a donation to charity and was wondering how much I should give, it would not help me much to be told that generosity consisted in giving neither too much nor too little. I need to decide how much to give in this situation. That is why I said above that Aristotle's analysis of virtue would serve as a rule of thumb for people not yet mature enough to make judgements of their own. Such people could act from well-formed habit or from a simple nostrum such as "Avoid extremes!", but a mature adult needs to make a judgement for herself. Accordingly, no account of ethics will be complete without some analysis of how we should make the many judgements that living ethically and successfully calls for. To this end, Aristotle now offers us an account of the "intellectual virtues" or skills of intelligence that we need to attain *eudaimoniā*.

When we are dealing with a purely theoretical matter, says Aristotle, we seek the truth. The purpose of our theoretical intellect is to discover facts and describe them correctly. So there is an inherent goal or a *telos* that our rational souls strive after: truth. Our thinking has the inherent tendency to get things right. But our intellect is not only concerned with theory and with facts. It is also concerned with action. The calculative part of the soul is what modern philosophers have come to call "practical reason". Just as the goal of theoretical reason is truth, the goal of practical reason is appropriate action in whatever circumstances we are in. And in so far as action involves desire as well as belief or intellect, appropriate action must also arise from correct desire (that is, desire that is appropriate to, and directed upon, a good object). And so practical reason involves reasoning that is true and desire that is right. Once again, Aristotle is giving us a holistic analysis of practical reason. It is not that reason is separate from desire and controls it, but rather that desire must be reasonable for the action that it motivates to be good. And so now Aristotle needs to explain how our desires and actions can come to be reasonable or rational. He does so by introducing the notion of "prudence" or "practical wisdom" (*phronēsis*).

Aristotle's concept of prudence (*phronēsis*) is central to his whole ethical philosophy. To understand it we need to consider Aristotle's concepts of "action" and "production". Production is typified by making something. As such its goal is that which is made. If I make a violin, then the goal of my activity is the production of that violin. My activity is completed, fulfilled or "perfected" by the violin that is the outcome of the production process. In contrast, an "action", in Aristotle's special sense of that term, is an activity for which the goal is the excellent doing of the activity itself. Suppose I play the violin and suppose further that I do so without an audience. What, then, is the objective of my activity? It is the making of beautiful music. But what is the making of beautiful music if not simply the excellent playing of the violin? Music is not a product (unless it is recorded or heard by an audience). It is gone the moment it is produced. The point of my activity is to play well rather than to make anything in the way of a definite product. So here the activity is its own reward, as it were. It has no goal except its own excellence in performance.

The intellectual skill or virtue that is particular to action understood in this way is prudence or practical wisdom (*phronēsis*). Normally (even in the ancient Greek it would seem) prudence is understood as the ability to make decisions that are to your own benefit. You act prudently when you do something that turns out well for yourself and for others for whom you might be concerned. But Aristotle builds a new level of meaning into this sense of the word. The violin player is benefiting himself, not in the way that a busker who collects money for playing well might, but by simply playing well. The better I play the violin in my bedroom the better I will feel about it and the more rewarding it will be for me. What sort of reward is this? It is not the monetary reward that the busker obtains. Nor is it honour or praise from others. These would be external goals. It is simply the fulfilment of my own effort at doing something that requires skill. Whenever I do something that takes some concentration, skill or commitment on my part, my doing it well will be a source of a sense of accomplishment and fulfilment for me. It will be a self-betterment in an ethical sense (although not in a moral sense; there is no direct question here of right or wrong or of moral enhancement or corruption). So the point of performing actions of this kind is to achieve this kind of self-fulfilment. In this sense I am acting in my own interest or prudently. And this requires knowledge or intellectual skill, not only because the activity is a skilful one, but also because it requires me to know what sorts of activities will be self-fulfilling for me in this way. Such knowledge will combine a high degree of self-knowledge with a broad knowledge of human nature and of social relationships.

It would illustrate Aristotle's point to consider a typically successful contemporary person. She might be highly productive in her work and in her life in the sense that she is producing many valuable outcomes or products for her company while also acquiring considerable wealth for herself, and yet she feels somehow unfulfilled. She has an inchoate sense that she is not doing what would be the best for her to do. She may have the knowledge and skills necessary to achieve success at her work, but she seems not to understand what her own inner needs are. She does not know how to achieve *eudaimoniā*. She lacks *phronēsis* and remains unhappy. So the sphere or field of the virtue of *phronēsis* – the area of life with which it concerns itself – is the human good. The prudent person is one who implicitly knows what is good for human beings – what would conduce to their fulfilment and thus *eudaimoniā* – and who acts intelligently in accordance with that understanding.

> What remains, then, is that it [prudence] is a true state, reasoned, and capable of action with regard to things that are good or bad for man.
> Aristotle, *Nicomachean Ethics*, 1140b4–6

There is an interesting point to note about Aristotle's distinction between action and production. The point of production is the product, whereas the point of an action is the doing of that action well. But a single activity can be both. Take the making of a violin. In so far as the point of that activity is the violin, it is a case of production. But we can also imagine the craftsman taking great pride in the excellence and care with which he makes his violins. We can imagine him doing his best and improving his skills and concentrating on every smallest detail of his craft. This will be highly satisfying for him and lead to great fulfilment. Even if the violin is destroyed soon after it is made, it will still have been a rewarding activity for him. And so making the violin can be an action in Aristotle's sense as well as a production. The violin maker can be exercising prudence as well as what Aristotle calls "technical skill" in this activity. The intellectual virtues in this case can be both the knowledge of how to make violins well, which is technical skill, and the implicit knowledge of what it is about human beings that makes such work so fulfilling, which is prudence.

> The wise man, then, must not only know all that follows from the first principles, but must also have true understanding of those principles.
> Aristotle, *Nicomachean Ethics*, 1141a17–18

I refer to prudence as implicit knowledge in order to distinguish it from Aristotle's concept of "wisdom" (*sophia*). We know from the fact that *sophia* is part of the etymology of the word "philosophy" that it is important to the ancient Greek thinkers. And Aristotle says explicitly that this is "the most finished form of knowledge" (1141a17). Wisdom is knowledge of those eternal things that the contemplative part of the soul concerns itself with. When it comes to human nature and ethics, the wise person has explicit and articulated knowledge of the principles the following of which would make us happy, whereas the prudent person has only implicit and practical knowledge of this: knowledge that allows him to make prudent judgements in particular situations even if he cannot always explain his reasons.

> Prudence apprehends the ultimate particular, which cannot be apprehended by scientific knowledge, but only by perception.
> Aristotle, *Nicomachean Ethics*, 1142a27–29

Aristotle also contrasts *phronësis* with "science" and "intuition" as they apply to the practical sphere of ethics and goodness. Whereas intuition apprehends the first principles by which we should live and science allows us to draw the correct logical implications from these principles by deduction, prudence is more focused upon the immediate and particular situation in which an agent finds him or herself. In this way prudence involves what Aristotle calls "perception". The prudent person has an implicit grasp of general principles. As a result, the distinctive intellectual skill that he displays is that he can be in a particular situation and immediately see what is ethically relevant in it. And, of course, he acts accordingly (because action flows directly from choice). What Aristotle is saying here is that it is not enough to know ethical principles. You could be a well-read and wise moral philosopher and be able to articulate and justify a great many important moral principles, but unless you see how these principles apply in everyday life, and act on them, it will all be so much empty rhetoric.

The link between these principles and action is forged by the ability to see what it is about a particular situation that calls upon you to act in accordance with a principle. It is no good knowing that you ought to be generous if you do not even notice the beggar on the street, or if you, on noticing the beggar, see him as a scruffy, work-shy layabout. It is how you see the situation that influences how you act and this "perception" is already ethically structured by your virtue. Even if you cannot explain your principles you could be virtuous if you see the world around you sensitively and act appropriately in response to what you see.

> First, then, let us say that wisdom and prudence, both being virtues – one of one part of the soul and the other of the other – must necessarily both be desirable in themselves, even if neither of them produces any result. Next, they do produce results: wisdom produces happiness, not as medical science produces health, but as health does. For wisdom is a part of virtue as a whole, and makes a person happy by his possession and exercise of it. Again, the full performance of man's function depends upon a combination of prudence and moral virtue; virtue ensures the correctness of the end at which we aim, and prudence that of the means towards it.
>
> Aristotle, *Nicomachean Ethics*, 1144a1–9

Aristotle alludes here to his division of the rational part of the soul into a calculative and a contemplative part. Prudence (*phronēsis*) is the highest virtue of the calculative part of the soul, whereas wisdom (*sophia*) is the highest virtue of the contemplative part. Prudence is concerned with action in the particular circumstances in which we find ourselves, with how we sensitively perceive those circumstances, and how much of ethical salience we see in them for ourselves and for others. In contrast, wisdom is concerned with the general and the universal. It is our articulate grasp of the principles and values that arise from our natures as human and social beings. It is by these values that we should live.

Aristotle thinks that "prudence" or "practical wisdom" (*phronēsis*) is the most important of the intellectual virtues. He contrasts it with yet another intellectual skill: cleverness. This is the quality shown by a cynical person who is very good at getting what he wants. He understands the system, notices the opportunities it gives him, avoids any illegalities or other problems, is quick in his reactions, and is very successful. But his goals are, arguably, not noble. All he wants is wealth for himself. He is clever but not prudent. Just as the bank robber who stares down his fear is not courageous because the goals on behalf of which he controls his fear are not noble, so the entrepreneur who uses all his wiles and cleverness to acquire wealth is not prudent. The goals that he is pursuing will not, Aristotle would argue, conduce to his *eudaimoniā*. They are not ethical. The positive point that Aristotle is making here is that prudence is an inherently ethical virtue. As he puts it "One cannot be prudent without being good" (1144a36). (Remember that "good" does not only mean "morally good" in the modern sense; it also means being good at being a human being, that is, living a human life well.)

Indeed, the point that Aristotle then goes on to make is that being prudent is not only a necessary condition for being good, it is also a sufficient condition. Anyone who is prudent will thereby be good. You may have a variety of natural dispositions or trained habits for doing the virtuous thing, but unless you can see in a situation that acting virtuously is what is called for, your apparently good action will only occur because of that habit or disposition. It will lack the motivation to goodness that perceiving the situation sensitively and seeing what you ought to do in it brings with it. So a mature adult (one who is no longer just acting from habit) needs prudence in order to be virtuous. You cannot be good without being prudent. Prudence is a necessary condition of being good. But there is more. Even if you do not have settled habits or natural dispositions to act virtuously, if you have prudence you will see what a situation demands and be motivated to do it. You will feel how self-fulfilling acting in that way is even if you are not inclined to act that way or even if you do not fully understand why you should act that way (as a person of wisdom does). In this event prudence will produce the virtuous outcome. In this way, prudence is sufficient for being virtuous. It provides the insight and the motivation for acting well. And so you cannot be prudent without being good.

> Thus we see from these arguments that it is not possible to be good in the true sense of the word without prudence, or to be prudent without moral goodness.
> Aristotle, *Nicomachean Ethics*, 1144b30–33

And it follows from this that prudence is all that a person needs in order to be virtuous. If you can evaluate any given situation in the light of what is ethically important in it and in the light of what would produce genuine happiness in yourself and others, then you will do the virtuous thing (provided there is no weakness of will, of course). In the absence of what Aristotle calls "incontinence", prudence is the whole of virtue. Although we can classify the virtues in the way that Aristotle does, using a variety of different names to designate different kinds of virtuous act in different kinds of situation, (generosity, courage, justice and so forth), they all boil down to prudence. They are all cases of a sensitive, insightful and sympathetic agent seeing what a situation demands and what would be fulfilling for him or her or the community to do in that situation and then setting about doing it. Prudence gives us the ability to judge what would be excessive in a particular situation and what would be deficient.

Of course, there is a chicken-and-egg problem here. If prudence is necessary and sufficient for acting virtuously, and prudence consists in a sensitive and perceptive (that is, virtuous) awareness of what is ethically important in a practical situation, then how can I come to be prudent? Would not being prudent consist in already being virtuous? Only a good person would see what was ethically required in a situation. Only a good person would see the beggar as deserving of help. And so she would need to be good already in order to see the good that she could do, and then do it. So where would the prudence come from that is necessary for acting well? In order to answer this question it is important to see that Aristotle is talking about mature individuals here. Such individuals will already have been trained in the habits that constitute the virtues of character. They will already have developed the habits of acting in appropriate and moderate ways in relation to desires. Add to this the influence of education and rational discussion of the principles by which we should live, and mature persons will be able to move from a virtuous motivation based on the habits that upbringing has given them to a motivation based on sensitive awareness of the particular situation. Prudence builds on virtue that is already there in an unreflective form and gives it new motivational strength and autonomy. As a youth your virtue consisted in being well trained. As an adult, virtue builds on this and becomes based upon your prudent judgement. There may even be times when you judge that the appropriate response is one that is not like that of the well trained youth. One may, on occasion, go against convention or the social norms. But this can still be virtuous if it is based upon an ethically sensitive awareness of what matters in that situation. The importance of the intellectual virtues is that they constitute our autonomy as ethical agents.

The nature of happiness

The final book in Aristotle's text is about happiness (*eudaimoniā*). Although he has already given us a brief sketch of what happiness is in Book 1, it is in this final book of his treatise that he brings his whole theory to a rounded conclusion. Happiness is the crowning achievement of a well-lived and successful life. If the point of being ethical is that we should be happy, then a treatise on ethics should tell us what happiness is. One candidate as to what happiness is will be pleasure and enjoyment. Aristotle will discuss this thesis at some length before finding it inadequate. Another candidate is having friends. It is in these books that Aristotle shows the deep humanity and worldliness of his thought. As opposed to Plato's image of the philosopher or "lover of wisdom" as a solitary figure longing to escape from the vicissitudes of life so as to contemplate the eternal realities in a life of isolation from the everyday world, Aristotle acknowledges that a full and happy life involves having friends. One's friends are a kind of mirror in which one can see one's own virtue and they provide, in this way, a human milieu in which the goodness that one has developed in life is rewarded through the companionship of the equally good. The person who is successful in life and has acquired virtue is seen by Aristotle as still embedded in this world. And it is a very congenial world at that.

This focus on the world of our everyday existence is very important for Aristotle. Happiness or *eudaimoniā* is not something attained by seeking to depart from this life as Plato had suggested with his parable of the cave. It is to be found in life. Aristotle does not look upwards and away from the world in seeking the highest objects of knowledge and the deepest sources of virtue. He sees such objects and such sources as existing here on this earth. Finding them contributes to our happiness, but we do not need to seek them in a transcendent reality.

Yet, even though this is the major thrust of Aristotle's thought throughout the text, the final book of the *Ethics* seems to have a different focus. In this book Aristotle does seem to direct our attention away from this world in a way that is reminiscent of Plato. To understand Aristotle's position correctly will require a careful reading of his text.

The theme of Book 10 is *eudaimoniā* as the supreme Good which it is our inherent goal to pursue. Aristotle begins by rejecting the views of those who say this goal is pleasure. He argues that pleasure cannot be the supreme Good because we can make judgements about just how good or virtuous it is in particular circumstances. Because we can ask whether any particular pleasure is noble, selfish, dignified or ethical, we must be assuming that it is not an unequivocal good in itself. If it is only good provided that it be ethical in some way, and if it can be judged to be brutish, self-indulgent or excessive, then there must be a higher standard against which pleasures can be evaluated as good or bad. And if this is so then it cannot itself be the supreme Good. Then, in Section IV, Aristotle begins to develop his own view. He tells us that "pleasure perfects the activity" (1074b24). Pleasure is not part of the outcome of an activity so that it only comes into being when the activity is completed. It is not the product of an activity. Rather, it is an accompaniment of that activity when the activity is being done well. To call pleasure the "perfection" of an activity is to suggest that it is a phenomenological quality that that activity has for the agent when it is being performed well by that agent. The activity may take time (like playing chess because it has discrete stages) but the perfection of the activity (its being done well) is complete at any given moment. "Perfection" is not a measure of the outcome of the action but of the way it is performed. Once again, we can use the example of the game of chess to illustrate this. When we play chess there are at least two marks of success. The most obvious is to win. This is the outcome and it is not realized until the game is over. But the person who loses the game might also have had some success. He might have played better than he had ever done before. He might have used some new moves and learnt some new strategies. He might have ended up pleased with the way he played. But this is not an outcome in the same sense that a win is an outcome. The success is, in this case, something that was realized throughout the game rather than just at the end. He played well and this was a fulfilment of the goals of the game that transpired throughout the game. This is a "perfection" of the game. At any moment during the game, this perfection is being realized as the players play well.

We can also develop this thought in terms of our distinction between internal and external goals of an activity. Suppose you are playing in a chess tournament that has a prize of a thousand dollars. The external goal of playing this game of chess is winning the thousand dollars. This is not a goal that belongs to the game as such or that is defined in the rules of the game. In that sense it is "external" to the game. In contrast, playing well and outsmarting your opponent is an internal goal of the game. That is what the game is all about and what constitutes "playing well". Anyone who plays will have this as a goal; it is a goal that is "internal" to the game. Winning the game is best thought of as an internal goal in this sense. It is defined by the rules of the game and it is a goal that every player has to have in order to be genuinely playing. (However, it is also a little bit like an external goal in that it is a state of the game that only occurs at its end.) An external goal is one that is extraneous or inessential to it, whereas an internal goal is one that is achievable at every moment of the activity and is intrinsic to it. To do something well is to achieve an internal goal of the activity no matter what the outcome. In this sense, the "perfection" of an activity is the fulfilment of its internal goals.

Aristotle's point is that to enjoy an activity (or to take pleasure in it) is a fulfilment of the internal goals of that activity. It is a perfection of that activity. "Fulfilment" is a particularly apt word to use. I called it a "phenomenological quality" earlier, because enjoyment is an internal goal or perfection that is manifested by the way one experiences the activity. To enjoy an activity is to experience it as fulfilling the internal goals of that activity.

When Aristotle speaks of "pleasure" in this context he means the "perfection of an activity" in this sense. He even goes on to say that pleasure is a perfection of a whole life in this way. Although this is not saying that pleasure is a supreme Good (because it is subject to ethical appraisal) it is saying that it is a very important and essential quality of a well-lived life and should not, of itself, cause us any ethical qualms (as it might for a puritan). If an activity is good, then the pleasure one feels as one does it well is also good.

> Thus the pleasure proper to a serious activity is virtuous, and that which is proper to a bad one is vicious; for desires too are laudable if their objects are noble, but censurable if they are base.
>
> Aristotle, *Nicomachean Ethics*, 1175b27–30

In Section VI, Aristotle pulls all the threads of his discussion together in order to define the central concept of his whole thesis: "happiness" or *eudaimoniā*. It turns out that happiness is a larger-scale version of pleasure as we have just defined it. Happiness in this sense is a phenomenological quality that accompanies action. It is the fulfilment of the internal goal of that action (an action that is chosen for itself rather than for the sake of something else, as he puts it). But the focus is no longer on individual actions. Just as Aristotle had said in Book 1 that one swallow does not make a summer, so one action does not make a life. And one enjoyable activity does not constitute happiness. Happiness is to be thought of as a quality of an aggregation of actions over time where those actions make up a significant aspect or period in a life. So the "actions" of which we are speaking might be "being married" or "being an executive in a large company" or "being a housewife". Although not everything that you do in life will fall within such descriptions, such descriptions do capture a significant portion and focus of your life. And such ways of being, or career choices, have both external and internal goals. Although the fulfilment of the external goals (such as success or wealth) will give us what Aristotle calls "felicity", which increases our chances of being happy, happiness proper is the fulfilment of the internal goal of such a significant portion of our lives.

Another way in which Aristotle distinguishes *eudaimoniā* from other kinds of perfection of action is by the seriousness of the action. If an action is not serious (such as watching television, say, or having a kick with the football) its perfection is called "amusement". This is innocent enough, but it plays a subservient role in the pursuit of *eudaimoniā*. We may need some amusement to relax, but such amusement is not a constitutive part of *eudaimoniā* in the way that the performance of serious and virtuous actions is.

Again, Aristotle thinks it is distinctive of happiness that the actions that it perfects are those of a free and independent agent. Actions that are performed in obedience to someone else or under the pressure of necessity do not constitute *eudaimoniā*. This is why a slave cannot be happy. Making a similar point, Aristotle also says that the actions the perfection of which constitutes *eudaimoniā* are self-sufficient. What this means is that the finest actions do not involve being dependent on others for the supply of necessary equipment or resources. The cultural context in which Aristotle makes these remarks suggest that he has in mind the social situation of aristocratic males in the ancient Greek city-state. Such people were independent and autonomous and were not beholden to anyone else for the opportunities that life gave them. The ideal form of their life would be readily seen by Aristotle, who mixed with them, as the objectively best form of life for all and the style of life most likely to constitute *eudaimoniā*.

This is one of several points where Aristotle's thought is, perhaps, too closely tied to the conditions of his own social class. Aristotle should have been able to see that ordinary people, women and even slaves are capable of those fine forms of activity that lead to happiness. It only takes a slight modification of his theory to extend the opportunity for a fully fulfilling life to all human beings equally. The theoretical framework for such an extension is clearly there in Aristotle's concepts. It is only a pity that with an inessential observation about the "self-sufficiency" of actions leading to happiness, he seems to reduce the scope of his theory unnecessarily.

Yet another way in which Aristotle distinguishes *eudaimoniā* from other kinds of perfection of action is by the part of the soul that the action exercises. So, good exercises of the desiring part of the soul (desiring the right objects and to the right degree) are virtuous and important constitutive parts of *eudaimoniā*, but even finer are good exercises of the rational part of the soul. It is this thought that leads Aristotle to his next major point.

> If happiness is an activity in accordance with virtue, it is reasonable to assume that it is in accordance with the highest virtue, and this will be the virtue of the best part of us. Whether this is the intellect or something else that we regard as naturally ruling and guiding us, and possessing insight into things noble and divine – either as being actually divine itself or as being more divine than any other part of us – it is the activity of this part, in accordance with the virtue proper to it, that will be perfect happiness.
>
> Aristotle, *Nicomachean Ethics*, 1177a11–18

In Section VII, Aristotle sums up the trend of his preceding exposition in order to argue that contemplation is the finest activity available to human beings and thus the activity most fully constitutive of *eudaimoniā*. The contemplative man is the happiest man of all.

There are some problems raised by this argument. First, the image that Aristotle projects in these arguments is that of leisured Greek aristocratic men engaged in an intellectual activity. It seems to be an activity confined to a particular class and gender. As I have already suggested, I do not think that this is a very serious problem because it would do no damage to the basic structures of Aristotle's arguments to extend his analyses in principle to women, working-class men and even slaves.

Secondly, a more serious problem is that it reverses the stress on activity that had been such a strong and progressive tendency in Aristotle's thought up until now. The importance that Aristotle gives to *phronēsis* arises from his recognition that the most important expression of virtue is in the life of action. And Aristotle sees action in holistic terms. He wants to show how our thinking and even our theoretical knowledge is bound up with our active lives and comes to expression in them. He said in Book 6 that, although the life of theory and wisdom is important, it is not as important as being able to express our wisdom practically. Being well informed about theory is not as important as being able to act well in practical life. *Phronēsis* is more important than *sophia*. And yet here, in Book 10, he says the exact opposite. The life of practical virtue is not as worthy as the life of contemplation. It is happy only "in a secondary degree". Is Aristotle being inconsistent?

I think not. Although Aristotle does not say so in the text, I think Aristotle's treatise can be read as following the trajectory of a typical Greek aristocratic male life. The earlier books in the text talk about the virtues that pertain to the appetitive part of the soul and that need to be inculcated in the young by training. The first phase in the life of a young Greek male was that of being a soldier. A soldier needs discipline and self-control. And it is to the virtues relevant to that – especially courage, temperance and continence – that the text turns (and to which it returns in Book 7). The text moves on in Book 6 to talk about the virtues of the rational part of the soul and thus by implication (and implicitly) about the education that is needed for the young in order to turn them into autonomous adults able to make responsible decisions. A soldier does not need to make autonomous decisions; he just follows orders. But what does an autonomous adult in Greek life do? He was trained as a youth to be a soldier but he is now a citizen and a statesman. In the democracy of ancient Athens, everyone of mature age was entitled to participate in political decision-making and thus needed a high degree of practical wisdom. The practical man lives a political life and for this the virtue that is most needed is *phronësis*.

Aristotle's *Ethics* is a manual for living well that unfolds in accordance with the life stages of its audience. The first division of the work is directed towards youth and those who have responsibility for the young. The second division of the work is directed towards mature adults who make autonomous decisions. The third and last division, I would now like to suggest, is directed to older men who are retired. These men are no longer statesmen taking an active part in the politics of the city and, of course, they are no longer soldiers. What then is *for them* the most valuable way of living? The life of contemplation. If I am right in my interpretation, Book 10 does not contradict Book 6. Book 6 is meant for active citizens and statesmen whereas Book 10 is directed mainly at the elders of the city and suggests to them what would be the best form of life for them. Every community has the problem of how to live with its elderly. Whereas we might lock ours away in nursing homes, the Greeks gave them an important role in society and an important set of activities to engage in. They were to be the keepers of the collective wisdom and the interpreters of the ancient traditions. Just as with the elders in many tribal societies, the elderly men in ancient Athens were expected to be wise and to be able to explain and articulate the deepest beliefs of the community. So, for them, the best and most noble activity was that of contemplating the eternal verities and exercising wisdom. *Eudaimoniā* changes through the lifespan. For a young person *eudaimoniā* consists in the control of the passions and desires that good training gives him. For a mature adult building on the virtues of youth, *eudaimoniā* consists in practical wisdom and the social respect, responsibilities and admiration which that form of virtue brings with it. For the retired elderly *eudaimoniā* consists in studying eternal things and discoursing about them with others.

In a life taken as a whole *eudaimoniā* consists in fulfilling all those phases of a well-lived life at the stages in life that are appropriate for them. Just as *phronēsis* does not replace the virtues of character but builds on them, so the life of *theoria* does not replace *phronēsis* but builds on it. The fulfilment of all these modes of living constitutes *eudaimoniā* at the time in life that is suitable for it. So happiness, over a whole life, is a package of different perfections suited to the different phases of that life. Contemplation is therefore not the only activity that would make us happy.

We could even extend this point in a direction that Aristotle himself did not pursue. If happiness is constituted by different perfections of activities at different phases of a life, then it might also be constituted by excellent activity in different kinds of life. One could say, for example, that for a flute player happiness is the perfection of playing the flute. Here *eudaimoniā* would be the perfection of an artistic skill as exercised over the major part of a life. For a householder *eudaimoniā* might consist in the perfection of the activities associated with the home, be they nurturing the children, cooking the meals or tending to the needs of a partner. To the extent that any person lives life with a commitment to the goals internal to the predominant activities of that life and fulfils those goals well, they will achieve *eudaimoniā*. But does this apply to any kind of life: even that of a criminal?

I have said that Aristotle's text is not primarily concerned with what we today call morality, but it is not irrelevant to it either. The Western tradition has certainly read it as being important for our understanding of what we are morally obliged to do or not do. So how does this ethics of a well-lived life touch on issues of morality? Could *eudaimoniā* be achieved through the form of life of bank robbers and other criminals? Aristotle would want to say that a criminal or a morally corrupt person cannot be happy. Happiness is linked to virtue. As Aristotle had put it in Book 1: "the good for man [that is, *eudaimoniā*] is an activity of soul in accordance with virtue" (1098a17). The perfection of action that constitutes our happiness does not just consist in doing that action well, no matter what the action is; it also depends on the goodness of the action. An action is performed in accordance with virtue when it is in moderation in relation to the desires that are relevant to it, and with sensitive and rational awareness of what is important in the situation both for the agent and for others affected by the action. Such actions will thereby be inevitably morally good actions. A person of moderate desires and practical wisdom will not knowingly do a morally bad thing. A bank robber has an immoderate desire for money and has but little understanding of the limited role that money has in the living of a good or *eudaimon* life. And so, even though the focus of Aristotle's treatise is on how to be happy, it also teaches us to be moral since that is a prerequisite for being happy.

> Against those who cite instances of disreputable pleasures one may argue that these pleasures are not pleasant. They may be pleasant to person of an unhealthy disposition, but that does not compel us to believe that they are really pleasant (except to these persons).
>
> Aristotle, *Nicomachean Ethics*, 1173b20–23

A criminal is more likely to enjoy the product of his action rather than the inherent quality of his action. In the case of thieves, this product will be the pleasures of wealth. But the pleasures that come from ill-gotten gains are not likely to be noble ones that conduce to the internal fulfilment of the agent. Indeed, they are not even genuinely pleasant. And in any case, production is of secondary importance to action in our happiness. It is not what we achieve that matters so much as what we do and how we do it. It is the inherent perfection of our actions that constitutes our happiness and if the action is not performed for a noble cause, this perfection will be absent.

It has to be acknowledged that these arguments are a little weak given the importance of their conclusion. We would like to think that a person who has stolen money and got away with it cannot be happy but the evidence often contradicts us. Even though he should have seen the injustice of his action and has thus failed in the exercise of practical wisdom, he might well be genuinely enjoying the pleasures that his ill-gotten wealth has given him. And those pleasures might be noble ones, such as the enjoyment of high art and creativity. Aristotle's claim would be that, because it is not in accordance with virtue or the result of virtue, this enjoyment could not contribute to a genuine state of happiness. Stories of successful criminals whose consciences could give them no rest might support this view, but we can also imagine totally callous and immoral characters having no such qualms. Is Aristotle being overly idealistic?

My view would be that we consider this to be a strong objection because we are tied to a subjective and individualistic concept of happiness. We think that happiness consist just in the states of enjoyment or contentment of individuals. But Aristotle, like the ancient Greeks generally, thought in more objective and social terms. Happiness was a state that you were in by virtue not only of your internal condition of contentment, but also by virtue of the way you were actually living your life and of the judgements of others about you. If you were known to be a criminal then you would not be seen as a happy person because happiness was understood as the public condition of honour that you enjoyed by virtue of your life of virtue. To be deemed a happy man was a public judgement that others made about you just as much as it is a private judgement that you might make about yourself. And the public would not regard a criminal as a happy man unless they were as cynical as that criminal might be himself. To be judged a happy man was to be praised as an example of virtue. Even though Aristotle speaks of "the activity of the soul" he is not locked into the modern conception of the mind as a private space internal to an individual person. Your soul is manifested in the way you act. Action is a public event. And the perfection of your action is manifest in the way you live your life. If you do the wrong thing in order to gain some advantage you may achieve some internal satisfaction but you will not achieve happiness because one measure of your happiness, in the ancient Greek conception, is your reputation and your honour. If happiness in the sense of *eudaimoniā* is the inherent goal of human existence, it would not be inappropriate to include in it our standing in the sight of others. Even contented criminals do not enjoy such standing. Ethics has to do with how we regard one another as much as with how we stand in relation to abstract moral norms.

Summary and conclusion

Aristotle's theory of ethics provides a powerful contrast to the tradition of moral theory that gave rise to the ethics of duty and provides important insights into what is at issue in living well. It can be summarized in the following points.

- Aristotle's understanding of "ethics" has more to do with what makes life worth living than with obedience to the moral law. Given that human beings have purposes built into their very mode of being, virtue is whatever helps us achieve those purposes.
- Aristotle has identified as parts of the soul the four levels of existence the fulfilment of which constitutes our happiness.
- Aristotle distinguishes between "virtue of character" and intellectual virtues, based on our natural abilities, where the former are developed by training and the latter are developed by education.
- Aristotle's theory becomes normative in that he regards certain behaviours, especially those that relate to pleasure, as worthy of human beings but other behaviours as not worthy. The reason that one *should* be virtuous is that it is honourable to be so.

- Wisdom is an important intellectual virtue, but the most important of all is practical wisdom (*phronësis*) because it allows us to judge rightly what a situation calls for from us and to do it.
- The goal of virtue is to be happy in Aristotle's special sense of that term. You cannot be happy without being good.

Despite the appeal and importance of Aristotle's conception of ethics, it was overcome by subsequent intellectual movements in the West, especially that of Christianity. Detailing some of the crucial junctures in this intellectual history will allow us to understand how duty ethics came to dominate Western moral thought and also to understand the ideas that are being drawn upon today in order to better understand what virtue is and what its role in living a meaningful life might be. The purpose of Chapter 3 is to explicate these ideas: ideas that form a bridge between Aristotle's thinking and the postmodern condition in which we find ourselves today.

three

A brief history of virtue
from the Stoics to Levinas

Introduction

The history of moral thought in the West since Aristotle has been marked by a gradual reduction of the importance of the notion of virtue in favour of the notion of duty. Instead of seeing virtue as valuable in itself, people began to think of virtue merely as an aid to doing one's duty. This occurred under the influence of two leading ideas put forward by Plato: that we should live our lives under the guidance of transcendent realities; and that the faculty by which we could become aware of these realities was reason. Plato suggested that Goodness and Justice, for example, were not just concepts but actual realities, knowledge of which would lead us to act well, and that we would gain this knowledge by controlling our desires and emotions. Our knowledge connects us to these higher realities even as our bodies live in a cave of darkness and obfuscation. Human beings have their feet in the mud of this earth and their intellects in a higher reality. Even though we are imprisoned in this worldly, fallible, finite and vulnerable existence, our thinking can take us into a realm of perfection and godly ideals. The most noble and virtuous way to live, therefore, is to reject the things of this world and let our spirits soar towards the pure realm of ideas and perfections of which this world is merely a pale copy. This worldview comes down to us through our religious traditions as well as through the writings of many philosophers, beginning with the Stoics.

The term "Stoics" refers to a group of Greek-speaking philosophers ranging from Zeno of Citium (c.333–c.261 BCE), who taught in Athens, to Epictetus (*c.*55–135CE), who was a slave in the city of Rome. The word refers to a plaza in ancient Athens known as the Painted Colonnade or "Stoa", where Zeno taught. The Stoics suggested that human beings should model their lives on the eternal order of nature. If the gods ruled nature in accordance with justice then we should bring our lives into tune with it and accept with equanimity everything that happens. After all, everything that happens is meant to happen. If we suffer disappointment it can only be because we desire things to be other than they are. The best way to live, therefore, is to suppress the desires, extirpate the emotions and be guided by reason, which was the faculty that allowed us to see the order in nature. Although the term "virtue" was used to describe this state of equanimity, the structure of the thinking here was that of placing oneself under the aegis of a transcendent reality by controlling the passions rather than that of realizing and fulfilling every aspect of one's own nature, as it had been for Aristotle.

With the advent of Christianity and the writing of such philosopher-theologians as Augustine (354–430CE) and Thomas Aquinas (1224–1274), the rather vague conception of a transcendent reality that we should follow in order to live life well came to have a much more specific meaning: God – the God who had been seen in the Hebrew tradition as the giver of the moral law. Even though Augustine and Aquinas stressed the love of God as an appropriate feeling and motivation for acting well, the point of doing so now became that of obeying the law. Aquinas did follow the Stoics in saying that this law could be discovered in the nature of things by reason, but this law now acquired a new kind of normativity that came from God. Once again, the structure of moral thinking was that of using reason or faith to discover what it was our duty to do by looking towards a transcendent reality, while controlling the desires and emotions. Augustine had taught that love of things of this world could only distract us from the love of God whereas Aquinas spoke of God's grace giving us the virtues of faith, hope and charity, by which we could direct our thinking to higher things and away from this world.

The themes that emerge from these developments are that it is our duty to do God's will, or to live in accordance with nature conceived as a providential cosmic order, and that the virtues are states of character that help us to achieve this. The ideal of human excellence became that of a person who controlled or even suppressed her worldly desires and obeyed the laws that God or nature had laid down. Subsequent developments in moral theory, culminating in Kant, have reinforced these themes in ways that I have already explicated in Chapter 1. If virtue ethics is to be revived, therefore, it will need to re-establish two points that Aristotle made: first, that we are at home in this world (rather than being imprisoned in it, as Plato taught) and that we can find our perfection and fulfilment by living a fully human life without any necessary appeal to supernatural justifications or norms, and secondly, that the emotions are as important for this project as our reason and can guide us just as adequately towards living morally.

Another theme that becomes more important through the history of Western ethics is that of our relationships to other people. Aristotle's conception of virtue seemed to be all about individuals living well and fulfilling their potentials as rational human beings, although this did include having regard for others in a variety of ways. Aristotle sees every individual as essentially tied to their community and as making contributions to it through their prudence and other virtues. He stresses the virtue of justice, which involves giving every person their due. And his analysis of friendship highlights the importance of sociability and of our relationships with others. Nevertheless, Aristotle does not highlight our feelings of concern for others or our responsibilities towards them. The point of being virtuous is to attain one's own happiness. Ethics, as Michel Foucault has recently put it, was a "care of the self". The modern conception of morality as being primarily concerned about our responsibilities and duties towards others does not find expression in this philosophy. Nor do the Stoics talk about this much. For them the important thing is our own peace of mind. The Christian moral philosophers certainly stressed our duty to love others as we do ourselves, but this is for the sake of serving God and achieving our own eternal reward in heaven. The problem that this leaves us with is just how to conceive of our relationships to others – whether they are our friends and family or distant strangers – in ethical terms.

In this chapter I shall explore the work of David Hume, Friedrich Nietzsche and Emmanuel Levinas, who discuss the following questions:

- Is ethics a transcendent or a worldly matter?
- What is the relation between the emotions and reason in our ethical lives?
- How do we relate to others ethically?

David Hume

It is a long way from the religious worldview of Aquinas to the almost iconoclastic secularism of David Hume (1711–1776), a notable contributor to the Scottish Enlightenment. Hume insists that all sound knowledge must be based on direct experience and thereby calls into question not only such metaphysical speculations as theological pronouncements about the nature and will of God, but also any theories about an inherent and universal human nature based on the existence of a rational soul. Both God and the soul are metaphysical postulations of which we cannot have direct sensory experience and are therefore suspect bases for moral theory. Even if it were possible to attain certain knowledge about such matters, the propositions expressing that knowledge would tell us what *is* the case about, for example, human desires and tendencies, but this would tell us nothing about what we *ought* to do. To use a contemporary example, even if it were true that, because of their genetic shaping by evolutionary history, human males were inclined to be aggressive, it would not follow that they *ought* to be aggressive. Hume insists that you cannot deduce an *ought* statement from an *is* statement. So not only are the metaphysical and anthropological speculations of such moral theorists as Plato, Aristotle, the Stoics, Augustine and Aquinas not reliable as knowledge, but they are also irrelevant. Nothing can be deduced from them as to how human beings ought to behave. The basis for our moral norms will have to be found elsewhere.

Hume also calls into question the traditional moral psychology stemming from the ancient Greeks in which reason was assumed to be a power that should control desire and the emotions, which he refers to as "the passions". For Hume, reason is simply the ability to think logically. You are reasonable when you are logical. You are using reason correctly when you perform arithmetic calculations without error and when you deduce conclusions from premises according to the correct rules of logic. But this is just a matter of deriving correct data output from data input. By itself, this cannot tell us what we should do unless the input already says or implies what we ought to do. By itself, reason cannot ground any norms, imperatives, "ought" statement or virtue ideals. So if reason were to control the emotions by itself there would not be any values on behalf of which, or in pursuit of which, it would exercise this control. It would be like a computer taking control of your life. Unless that computer had goals or wanted to achieve some outcomes, it would be blind, no matter how rational its operations were.

> Reason is, and ought only to be the slave of the passions, and can never pretend to any other office than to serve and obey them.
>
> David Hume, *A Treatise of Human Nature*, ch. 63

Hume's basic insight is that reason is a tool that is used by our desires in order to get what they want. Our desires and feelings are the primary motivators of our actions. We use reason in order to calculate the best means for attaining what we want, but without wanting something first, our reason stands idle. We want things and then think about how to obtain them. To be virtuous we need to want to be virtuous rather than relying on reason to motivate us. If the primary issue in any moral theory is how we are to move from being only interested in ourselves and motivated to pursue our own desires to being concerned for others and willing to help them or respect their rights, then it is not reason that is going to motivate such a move. We need to want to help others or respect their rights in the first place. So Hume's answer to the question of what would be the basis of our moral norms is not reason, but our feeling of concern for others. He variously calls this feeling "sympathy", "affection" or "the sentiment of humanity".

> There is no spectacle so fair and beautiful as a noble and generous action; nor any which gives us more abhorrence than one that is cruel and treacherous.   David Hume, *A Treatise of Human Nature*, ch. 72

Hume argues that a virtuous person is one who has feelings of sympathy and concern for others. This feeling will allow such a person to approve of good deeds in themselves and in others and to disapprove of bad ones. What is it about a lie that elicits our moral disapproval? It is not reason considering just the logical inconsistency of such an act, but a dislike of deception or of seeing someone taken advantage of. If moral knowledge is based on experience rather than metaphysical speculation, then the experience Hume appeals to is that of our feeling of approval or disapproval for the actions that people perform. In this way morality does not have an objective foundation but a subjective one: our moral sentiments.

Of course, a bad person may feel approval for the bad actions he observes or enacts. In such people the mere feeling of approval may not be virtuous. Therefore, there must be some test that we can apply to judge which feelings of approval are morally good. Hume's answer to this problem is an early form of utilitarian thinking. We approve of those actions that lead to general happiness or *utility*. We would not be virtuous if we felt approval for actions that harmed others or caused social problems. But it is not pure reason that adjudicates this matter. It cannot be concluded from pure reason that we should care about others. Our concern that people not be harmed or society not disrupted is a concern that arises out of our general sympathy for others. Without such concern, we would not care what happened as a result of what people do. So the test by which we distinguish moral from immoral feelings is the conformity of those feelings with our more general feeling of sympathy for, and caring about, others. Hume's version of utilitarianism would not get off the ground unless he posited a positive moral motivation for that way of thinking.

> May it not thence be concluded that the *utility* resulting from the social virtues forms, at least, a *part* of their merit and is one source of the approbation and regard so universally paid to them?
> David Hume, *An Inquiry Concerning the Principles of Morals*, sec. II, pt. II

So the principles of morality are discerned by seeing what virtuous people approve of out of concern for the general good. Virtue is primary since it is the feelings of the virtuous that establish our knowledge of morality. It is not because it is in our own interests that we approve of moral actions but because we already have a concern for others. When he categorizes the virtues, Hume acknowledges that many virtues benefit their possessors: virtues such as temperance, sobriety, patience, constancy, perseverance and presence of mind. Other virtues benefit both others and the agent: including honesty, fidelity, industry, frugality and truthfulness. Even benevolence, which seems primarily directed towards the good of others, is also a source of satisfaction for the benevolent person. There are even some traits that have little utility and are still praised by others: traits such as good manners, ingenuity and modesty. But all of this is premised upon there being a common and universal sentiment of humanity. This sentiment is a sympathy for others that grounds our feelings of moral approval or disapproval. Although we are pleased when we act for the sake of others or observe such actions on the part of others, it is not a selfish motivation that leads us to act in such ways. Rather, it is our sentiment of humanity, or concern for others, that comes to expression in such actions or reactions.

The significance of Hume's subjectivist account of morality is that it reinstates the emotions as central to our lives. As opposed to the classical conception of reason as the faculty that should control our emotions so as to ensure our being moral, Hume recognizes the centrality of emotion. He has the rather generous view that most human beings have essentially benevolent feelings towards one another and argues that morality is the systematic expression of these feelings. Moreover, Hume sees morality and virtue as thoroughly secular phenomena. It is not based on any metaphysical ideas about the ability of our pure reason to discern the Good, God's commands, or the rational order of nature. Moreover, God has no role in grounding or enforcing moral norms. Virtue consists in living in harmony with our humane sentiments rather than in obeying the moral law.

Friedrich Nietzsche

If Hume's view of humanity was an optimistic one, that of Friedrich Nietzsche (1844–1900) may seem the very opposite. Rather than assuming that human beings are benevolently disposed towards each other, Nietzsche suggests that the basic motivation that drives human beings – and, indeed, all living beings – is what he calls "will to power". This is a drive or an instinct for self-assertion and competitiveness. Every living thing wants to do more than merely survive or be contented; it wants to excel, to be better than others of its kind, to dominate and to appropriate its place in the world for itself. Any form of subservience or humility is antithetical to its nature. Striving and overcoming are the very deepest motivators of all living things. For creatures such as ourselves, who are self-conscious, this overcoming and striving is directed against ourselves as well as others. We strive to overcome our own laziness and our desire for comfort. We seek to overcome our reliance upon those myths and unfounded beliefs that give us comfort in life and assure us of providential guidance towards cosmic justice. We seek to overcome the false consolations of theories that purport to give us certainty, including metaphysical theories about God or human nature.

Rather than subscribe to the classical view of human nature that posits a faculty of reason with the task of controlling a faculty of desire, Nietzsche sees human beings as dark, complex and multi-layered beings in whom desires and considerations of many kinds compete with each other for dominance and control. Desire and reason are not distinct. Rather, we are subject to drives and inclinations that are both rational in the sense of being effectively and cognitively directed towards a goal and desirous in the sense that they seek what they want. Each of them pursues its own goals and many are not even apparent to our powers of reflection and self-knowledge. For Nietzsche, what Kant and earlier philosophers had called the will is not a separate faculty that orders our desires in the light of reason, but merely the most dominant of our motivations and drives on any given occasion. Will to power is the energy of all of these anarchic little wills as they (that is, we) strive for dominance over each other and over the worldly things we come into contact with. Among these wills there might well be some that are benevolent or that are forms of the sentiment of humanity, but there will be competitive and aggressive wills as well. The deepest and most fundamental of them will be the will to affirm oneself as separate from, and better than, others.

> In all willing it is absolutely a question of commanding and obeying, on the basis, as I have said already, of a social structure composed of many "souls": on which account a philosopher should claim the right to include willing as such within the field of morality: that is, of morality understood as the theory of the relations of dominance under which the phenomenon "life" arises.
> Friedrich Nietzsche, *Beyond Good and Evil*, para. 19

Of course, it might be that none of this is true. How would we find out whether it is? Is it a matter that can be decided by scientific methodologies? Why would we even want to be certain about such a matter? If you preferred Hume's optimistic view, which gives predominance to the sentiment of sympathy, or if you preferred Aristotle's view that our souls were pre-eminently rational, how would you argue your case? And how would you justify the Stoic belief in a rational order in nature or the Christian belief in a God who inscribed the moral law on to our human natures? None of these grand theories are provable and Nietzsche does not pretend that his alternative is any more provable. Such theories, he says, are stories that we tell ourselves to give meaning to our lives. We need some overarching metaphysical view in order to make sense of human life. This world is a terrible place. Natural disasters happen, people attack and rob each other, we wage wars, half the world starves while the other half lives in luxury and people die without justice. We need stories to make sense of all this and to make our miserable lives meaningful. Plato and many religions direct our attention away from this world and posit a glorious beyond that we should strive for and seek to attain after our deaths. In this way, the world will not matter so much. Aristotle urges us to live within the finite parameters of human existence and to moderate our desires and direct them through reason. The Stoics urge us to extirpate our emotions so as to avoid disappointment and grief. Aquinas says we are destined for eternal life. Hume says most of us are motivated to create as much happiness and harmony on this earth for ourselves and others as is humanly possible. Anticipating the concept of hermeneutics, Nietzsche says that all these beliefs are consolations. Their value lies not in their truth, which cannot be proven, but in the degree to which they can make our lives liveable.

Nietzsche's own view is no more certain. But it does have one advantage. It is more honest. Whereas the earlier views gilded the lily by giving supernatural qualities to humanity, Nietzsche's view hides nothing of our brutishness from us. Moreover, many of the earlier views expressed a hatred of this worldly life of ours. The task for humanity was to reject the world in favour of an idealized or post-mortem existence in a supernatural realm of perfection. Nietzsche not only accepts humanity with all its warts, but also celebrates the worldly, finite and fallible existence that we have here on earth.

So how should we live? What is it to live life well, given that we are driven by will to power? We should become who we are. We should realize our potential. We should give expression to our will to power. We should be honest about what lies within us. But would giving expression to this competitive, aggressive and self-affirming way of being lead to a life in tune with morality? That depends on what you mean by "morality", says Nietzsche. If your conception of morality is part of that other-worldly, rationalistic, optimistic and benevolent story that we tell ourselves to give us comfort and a promise of a just reward, then it may seem not. But if your conception of morality is that it is itself an expression of will to power as lived in a finite and fallible world, then it may well be.

And there are such conceptions of morality. Nietzsche calls one of them "master morality". It is the style of life of a type of person who is not afraid to express their will to power. Such a person will dominate others whether by force of personality or by force of arms. Such a person will glory in the company of other strong types and will be dismissive of weak and miserable types. As cultures and societies evolve through history, such types of person will come to dominate and to exercise social power. They will be the warriors, the conquerors and the aristocrats. They will not stoop to the common people and they will not fear suffering and death. They will not bear grudges or harbour resentment because they will have confidence in their own power and excellence. Their only fear will be that their type will degenerate as a result of luxury, preservation of the weak or self-indulgence. For this reason they will direct their power towards their own self-control and self-formation as well as towards the maintenance and growth of their prowess.

> There is *master morality* and *slave morality* … In the former case, when it is the rulers who determine the concept "good", it is the exalted, proud states of soul which are considered distinguishing and determine the order of rank. … The slave is suspicious of the virtues of the powerful: he is sceptical and mistrustful, *keenly* mistrustful, of everything "good" that is honoured among them …   Friedrich Nietzsche, *Beyond Good and Evil*, para. 260

Nietzsche contrasts the masterly type and their outlook on life with what he calls "slave morality". This is the outlook of the weak. If you are poor and miserable and have no ability to defend your own interests, then you will hate those who are self-confident and powerful. You will hate them because you fear them. And you will call their powerful deeds evil. You will try to find comfort in numbers. The weak band together in order to defend themselves against the strong. In this way you will create a herd mentality fuelled by hatred, fear and resentment. You will tell yourselves stories to comfort yourselves and those stories will become especially effective if they celebrate your weakness. Any story that blesses the weak and tells them that they will inherit the earth or that praises those who turn the other cheek will be stories that you cling to. You will cling to a God who allows himself to be crucified. What greater celebration of weakness and humility could there be than that? Indeed, so successful would such stories be that they even impress the masterly types. For all their strength and power, they might come to feel bad about exercising their might. They will voluntarily give up their arms and join the slave types in their worldview. And in this they will be conquered. And so the mentality of slaves has actually come to dominate in our Western cultures through the Christian religion. Humility and weakness have triumphed. The irony is that this very triumph demonstrates that, for all its celebration of weakness and humility, slave morality is just as much an expression of will to power as master morality is. It could not have won the day if it were not.

Does this mean that master morality and slave morality are on an equal footing in terms of value? No, says Nietzsche; master morality is to be preferred. It is more honest. It acknowledges and celebrates that it is an expression of will to power whereas slave morality hides this from itself. Slave morality pretends to be humble even as it dominates its rival. It is powerful but dishonestly hides this from itself by telling a story that celebrates weakness and subservience. Nietzsche considers that moral theory, in its creation of a concept of morality that stresses duty and obedience, is party to this dishonesty.

> Honesty – granted that this is our virtue, from which we cannot get free, we free spirits – well, let us labour at it with all love and malice and not weary of "perfecting" ourselves in *our* virtue, the only one we have.
> Friedrich Nietzsche, *Beyond Good and Evil*, para. 227

In contrast, Nietzsche advocates the "free spirit" that arises from the acknowledgement of will to power. Nietzsche's advocacy of a higher type of human being does not rest with the masterly type. He thinks this type of person, who could be exemplified by the great conquerors of history as much as by the schoolyard bully, should be overcome just as much as the slave type should be overcome. In their place there should emerge a noble type of person, a "free spirit", a type who overcomes the spiritual limitations of modern Europeans. This "person who overcomes" or *übermensch* will acknowledge the driving force of will to power, will be wary of metaphysical and philosophical theories that give us false consolation, will accept that whatever philosophical theories they propound themselves will be just such theories, will not seek to aggrandize themselves by feeling a false pity for the weak, and will respect others as equals if they are worthy of it. These noble figures will direct their will to power upon themselves so as to make their own lives into a work of art. They will introduce order into the chaos of their motivations: an order that is at once aesthetic and ethical. Instead of being "good" where this is defined as not being such as to inspire fear in the weak, they will be noble. Instead of avoiding sin, they will be grand. Instead of merely avoiding wrongdoing, they will be honourable. They will be honest and forgiving. They will be generous rather than resentful, confident rather than fearful, self-affirming rather than humble. Their virtues will be the product of commitment rather than obedience.

The greatest test for noble and free spirits will not be their concern or sympathy for others but their ability to accept life as it is. In paragraph 341 of his book *Joyful Wisdom* (often translated as *The Gay Science*), Nietzsche draws a fascinating scenario in order to illustrate this high level of spiritual virtue. Imagine that your life, as you were living it, with all its joys, hardships, triumphs and disappointments, were to be repeated exactly as it is for ever and ever: no change, no variation and no opportunity to go back on anything and do it differently. Every last detail, event and thought would be repeated exactly as you have experienced it and can reflect on it, for all eternity. Could you accept this? Could you celebrate it and embrace it? If so, you are a free spirit. You are the anti-Plato. You are so accepting of your worldly existence in the cave that you do not think it worthy of yourself to want to escape from it.

> My formula for greatness in a human being is *amor fati*: that one wants nothing other than it is, not in the future, not in the past, not in all eternity. Not merely to endure that which happens of necessity, still less to dissemble it – all idealism is untruthfulness in the face of necessity – but to *love* it …
> Friedrich Nietzsche, "Why I am so Clever", *Ecce Homo*, para. 10

This is virtue as self-affirmation and as acceptance of worldly existence. There is no reference here to any kind of transcendental reward for being moral or to any kind of life after death. There is courage in the face of the cosmic meaninglessness of life and the inevitable suffering that this world brings. There is a "tragic" outlook that refuses to seek justice at the hands of a providential God or of a vengeful human intervention. Bad things happen, that is all there is to be said. There is honesty in not accepting the consolations of metaphysics or of optimistic humanism. There is self-discipline in the struggle to bring order to your motivations and create an artistic structure to your life. There is the overcoming of the struggle between the powerful and the weak so as to move into a mood of respect for others for who they are. And there is pride.

Nietzsche is reinstating the pagan virtues that had been overwhelmed by Christianity. Instead of Aquinas's faith, hope and charity, we have pride and authenticity. Instead of loving one's neighbour as oneself, one loves oneself and this love reflects on to one's neighbour. Instead of Hume's sympathy, self-affirmation is all. Instead of moral theory declaring a universal and objective set of moral norms, we have free individuals affirming their own values as expressions of their noble outlook on life. Instead of a concept of nature or of the cosmos as rational, just or providential, there is the acceptance of human suffering as an inevitable aspect of human existence. The free spirits love fate and can accept whatever happens on this earth. This is their virtue. This new list of virtues expresses the self-affirmation and self-confidence that arises from will to power. But how can this way of thinking accommodate our virtuous concern for others?

To answer this question we need to make a new beginning and consider the notion of "character". This notion is fundamental to virtue theory. It is most usually thought of as the pattern of behaviour and response that arises in an individual on the basis of what that individual will have experienced in the way of upbringing, habit-formation and self-reflection, along with the genetic endowments that contribute to that individual's personality. Bernard Williams speaks of our motivations going "all the way down" to our characters. But, apart from our genes, what is it that lies within us as the basis of our characters? Of what are our characters the expression? What is it that is shaped by our upbringing and our own reflective efforts at self-improvement? Hume suggests that at least one of the fundamental motivations at the core of our being is sympathy for others, or the sentiment of humanity. In sharp contrast, Nietzsche proposes his concept of will to power. Following this train of thought into the fundamental levels of our characters, many continental philosophers of the twentieth century explore our "primordial mode of being" to see whether it makes ethics possible. What do I mean by this?

The metaphor of depth in the preceding paragraph should not lead you to think that "primordial" means "deepest", as if I was trying to identify the deepest and darkest recesses of our motivations in the way that a psychoanalyst might. "Primordial" is better understood as meaning "most taken for granted". Let us use Hume's theory to explicate this. Hume seems to be saying that we have within us a deep feeling of sympathy for others, a feeling that is expressed in benevolent actions on the part of virtuous people. This explanation uses the metaphor of depth. But we could also explicate his view by suggesting that everyone sees another person as always and already someone to be treated with sympathy and kindness. Because of the distortions that bad upbringing or bad motivations might introduce, some people might not give expression to this way of seeing others, but it is there for most of us as an inescapable lens through which other people are seen. We do not see trees and bicycles as things to be treated with kindness, but that is, from the very first, how we see people. Our very perception of people is structured with such a humane outlook. We would need to overcome this *prima facie* impression if we were to act viciously towards them. The point that I am making here is that the term "primordial", which many continental philosophers use when describing human reality, need not refer to anything deep and hidden, but rather to the first, or *prima facie*, way in which the world appears to us. This is "hidden" only in the sense that it is so common and obvious that we seldom notice it explicitly. We take it for granted that others appear to us in our world as persons that we care about in a way that we do not care about mere things.

Continental philosophers use the phrase "mode of being" to refer to the way in which a particular entity exists. It is easiest to illustrate this with an inert item. Take the pen that you may be holding as you read this book. What is its mode of existence? It exists just in itself. It is what it is, and has been made to be what it is by a manufacturer of pens. It cannot change its own being in any way. The only changes that can occur in it are changes brought about by causal influences from outside it. You might drop it and stand on it. That will certainly produce a change, but it will be a change that is inflicted on it from the outside. It can do nothing for itself by itself. It is simply there as a "thing". The most fundamental feature of the mode of being of a thing is that it occupies space and time and is part of a causal chain of events. Causes impact upon it and it, in its turn, has causal effects on other items. For example, it leaves traces of ink on paper when pushed around by your hand. Beyond that it is passive.

This contrasts starkly with the mode of being that you and I enjoy. We are active. As Nietzsche suggests, we are pure dynamism seeking to express ourselves in the world. We are constantly shaping and reshaping our own identity. Although this is not something we notice in the case of everyday and routine actions, our every action is formative of who we are. To the extent that those actions are based on explicit or implicit decisions that we are making, we create our own character and identity. So our mode of being is that of self-making. We make ourselves who we are. Although it is true that there are a myriad of influences upon us that shapes this process of self-making, and while it is true that our natural endowments and historical situation constitute constraints on what we can become, it is our own energy and our own initiative that, working within those constraints, ground our identity and selfhood. Our lives are a project for us. We constantly look forwards and pursue goals. We have plans and aspirations. Although we suffer disappointments and setbacks from a world that does not always bend to our will, what we become is the product of our striving and initiative in interaction with the world and with others. Accordingly, unlike the mode of being of a thing such as a pen, our mode of being is that of striving, being creative and self-making. If we did not enjoy such a mode of being we would simply have our identity defined for us by our circumstances and by others. Our characters are the repository of those efforts at self-making and the base from which new initiatives can be taken. Using the metaphor of depth, we could say that this creative mode of being, which continental philosophers call "existence" and which I prefer to call our "self-project", lies beneath the level of our characters. But if we used the term "primordial", we could say that before we even reflect on our own experience and on the way we live our lives our existence is always already marked by a striving for self-realization, and our lived world is always already perceived as a situation in which we seek to fulfil ourselves. *Prima facie*, some things in the world will be seen as helpful and other things will be seen as frustrating in relation to the self-project that is our primordial mode of being. This is so commonplace that we seldom notice it and we imagine that we see things as neutral objects with the same meaning for everyone.

This stress on our own self-project raises the central ethical problem that Nietzsche and the existential tradition of philosophy that he partly inspired has left us with: the problem of other people. Given that my mode of being is that of being a self-project – that of constantly defining my own identity in a world that may often not be hospitable to my creativity and independence – the presence of others in my world presents itself as a problem. Jean-Paul Sartre (1905–80) elucidates this point with some nicely drawn literary scenarios. In one of them he imagines a man relaxing in a quiet corner of a park. He is enjoying the sight of the trees and plants and the sounds of birds and a distant fountain. He has, as it were, appropriated that portion of the world as his own. He is the centre of it and, for the time being and from his perspective, it is there for him. It is his world and his park. But then another man enters that space. He is taking a relaxed stroll and also enjoying the sights and sounds. All at once the first man no longer "owns" that portion of the park. He is now not its centre and he has to share it with an intruder. Both men are appropriating the park into their own existence. Although we know that we should not feel intruded upon in this way and although we feel that the other person has a perfect right to be there and that we should share the space with them, Sartre suggests that our first and most primitive response will be to feel displaced from the centre of what we had taken to be our own world and to feel intruded upon. Sartre concludes from this that the most primordial form of our relationships with others involves our contesting the occupation of the world with them. Human beings are always intruding upon one another and competing to preserve their personal space. But if this is an aspect of our primordial mode of being, it is hardly a promising basis for ethical relationships with others.

Sartre heightens his argument when he draws a further scenario. In this vignette I am engaged in looking through a keyhole (the essential point about this example is that I am engaged in a socially disapproved activity) when I hear someone behind me and sense that they are observing me in this compromising position. I immediately feel myself being labelled as a peeping Tom and I feel both embarrassed and annoyed at being caught. The lesson that Sartre draws from this story is that other people put labels on me and thus define my identity with scant regard for how I would like to see myself. While this scenario is of a somewhat dramatic nature, Sartre maintains that such processes of being made into an identity for others go on constantly. It is an inescapable aspect of social life that others impose classificatory categories on me in one way or another. I am made by the way others see me into a white male, a university academic, a husband, an Australian and so forth. More specifically, I may be thought of as intelligent, lazy, strange-looking, loyal or interesting. Some of the labels that are imposed on me may be flattering, but others will be less welcome. Whatever categories and valuations are imposed on me, however, it is my central quest as an individual, says Sartre, to maintain my own freedom and authenticity in the face of this objectifying process that stems from the way others see me. My authenticity is my refusal to accept passively the labels that others put on me. Whatever I am, either in the eyes of others or in my own eyes, must be of my own making. It must be an expression of my own self-project. It must be my own creativity and my own existence that comes to expression in my character and in my identity. In Nietzschean terms, it must be my own will to power that grounds who I am. Once again, the ethical implication of this way of thinking will be clear. Other people are a threat to my authenticity. Given that the mode of being that constitutes the core of my self is self-project, I must constantly resist the ways that others seek to impose an identity upon me. As Sartre famously puts it, "Hell is other people". Given that ethics is concerned with how I treat other people as well as with how I live my own life, this doctrine made Sartre's various attempts at creating a theory of ethics that would embrace other people very problematical.

Having identified a level of analysis that is more primordial than the concept of "character", post-Nietzschean continental writers have initiated a new way of theorizing ethics and, more specifically, a new way of explicating the notion of virtue as an aspect of the inner life of ethical agents. However, they have, at the same time, made it difficult to attribute ethically positive characteristics to this mode of being. As we have seen, Hume attributes to our human natures a basic sentiment called "sympathy" that has ethically positive characteristics built into it. If I could explicate this using existential categories I could suggest that Hume thinks that the mode of being of human beings includes a quality of sympathetic concern for others. On this view, our caring about other people and our aptitude for being affected by their suffering would be a primordial feature of the very way in which we experience the world rather than a characteristic that we might acquire or not during the course of our upbringing. The key difference between what Hume actually says and what this existentialist version of his view would suggest is that the latter makes sympathy a necessary feature of our mode of being as human beings. Whereas one of the central problems that commentators found in Hume's doctrine of sympathy was that it posited a *contingent* feeling as the basis of our ethical responses – a feeling that we may or may not feel, depending on circumstances or on the formation of our characters – the existentialist notion of a mode of being is offered as a *necessary* feature of the way we are. It follows that if we could find an existentialist conception that would be attributable to all human beings no matter what their contingent circumstances and that would do the theoretical work that Hume's notion of sympathy does in his conception of virtue, then we would have provided a solid theoretical grounding for a virtue conception of ethics. The problem is that the Nietzschean tradition of thought as developed by Sartre and other existentialists gives primacy to the self-affirmation of the self as the centre of that self's world and thereby does not present an ethically positive conception of our primordial relationships with others.

Emmanuel Levinas

This is the problem to which the French philosopher Emmanuel Levinas (1906–95) can give us a solution. Levinas's writing is complex and difficult and I can offer only a selective exposition of his views here. Moreover, he does not offer us an ethics in the sense of a set of prescriptions as to what we should do or what traits of character would count as virtuous. What he does offer us is a philosophical understanding of human existence in which that existence is seen as primordially ethical in character. Whereas Sartre had assumed that we are beings for whom the way in which we appropriate the world to ourselves when we perceive it extends to everything in that world, including other people, Levinas suggests that it does not extend to the face of another person.

Let us try to understand that suggestion more fully by taking a few steps back from interpersonal relations and considering our knowledge of the world. The way in which philosophers have traditionally understood knowledge and perception is to suggest that we assimilate things into our cognitive schemes. It is as if we impose categories and classifications on things in order to integrate them into our familiar world. We cognitively take possession of what we perceive and know. I do not mean by this that we literally or legally own them, of course. I mean that we assimilate what was previously unknown and therefore beyond our ken into a lived environment in which everything has its place and its relation to me. Once again, we can use your pen as an example. Whether or not you legally own the pen, the key point is that it is a familiar item in your world. If you are sitting in your study, then your desk, the books in front of you, the poster of a pop star on your wall and even the buildings that you see through your window are all a familiar environment to you. This environment contains things that you use and also things that are not your legal possessions but that are familiar parts of "your" world. You gaze upon it as your own domain. This was, of course, Sartre's point in relation to the park. The very processes of cognition, of making sense of the world, involve your imposing your concepts and categories upon it and thereby appropriating it as *your* world.

But now imagine yourself having dinner with a person you are very close to. Once again you are in a familiar environment. As far as you are concerned you are assimilating this world of the restaurant to yourself. But what of your companion sitting opposite you at this candle-lit table? Do you also assimilate them into your world? As you gaze at their face and into their eyes, do you appropriate them into the lived world of familiar objects that constitutes your known and comfortable environment? Levinas would say no. He would insist that the face of the other person, and particularly their eyes (traditionally thought of as the "windows to the soul") are not assimilable in this way. They are a mystery. They are infinite in the sense of being ungraspable in the cognitive categories with which we appropriate our lived world. They are beyond our ken. Levinas is alluding to more than the important point that people are hard to get to know. Everyone seems to be keeping their own natures hidden within themselves. Indeed, the closer we are to someone the harder they seem to be to know. The spouse you might have lived with for many years continues to be a mystery to you. All of this is relevant, but Levinas is appealing to the very moment at which you look into that person's face. What you see there has such depth and mystery as to forever escape your cognitive grasp. You cannot assimilate it. You must let it be what it is.

> The face is present in its refusal to be contained. It is neither seen nor touched – for in visual or tactile sensation the identity of the I envelops the alterity of the object, which becomes precisely a content.
>
> Emmanuel Levinas, *Totality and Infinity*, 194

But this is not experienced as a problem to be overcome or as a threat to your own authenticity or selfhood. It is experienced by you as an opening on to something wonderful. It is experienced by you almost as a mystical rapport with something of infinite depth. (One can only speak in metaphors here since the hypothesis is that the other is unattainable through the categories of understanding.) And this changes the quality of your own being. Rather than now being the Nietzschean self-affirmer or the existential self-project, you become an openness to the mystery of the other. This is not, of course, a stance taken consciously or as the result of a decision. It is simply your mode of being as transformed by the presence of the other person. Your primordial comportment towards the world is now no longer that of a self-project bent on making and affirming your own identity and on appropriating the environment as your own lived world; it is that of reverence and wonder in the presence of the mystery of the other. And this comportment or stance always already has an ethical quality.

I can illustrate this last point by using a much more mundane example than the intimate candle-lit dinner. Imagine yourself buying a railway ticket from an automatic vending machine. Here you are engaging in an interaction with a machine. As such the action falls clearly within that familiar world that you have appropriated to yourself through the way you understand and live in that world. You are the centre of this world and you do not need to respond to the machine as anything other than a thing that is there for you. But now imagine yourself buying the train ticket from a station attendant seated in a ticket booth. From a pragmatic or functional point of view the exchange is not different from the previous one. You are obtaining a ticket in exchange for money. However, there is a qualitative difference. This difference is marked by the etiquette of saying "please" and "thank you" and, perhaps, of exchanging some remarks about the weather. These words add nothing to the functionality of the exchange but they are important in that they mark your acknowledgement of the other as a person rather than a machine. The very presence in that booth of a person elicits in you a courteous and pleasant response. Although hardly a dramatic moment in your life, this response is an expression of a primordial ethical comportment that marks your mode of being as ethical. Without any deliberate thought, you acknowledge and respect the mystery of that other person in those simple gestures.

It may be objected that such a courteous response to a station attendant is the result of your having a well-formed character rather than its being an expression of your primordial mode of being as open to the other. It certainly seems to be true that there are some people who are so rude as to buy a ticket from a person with the same mechanical aloofness as they show when using a machine, and this might show that it is a matter of upbringing and character formation that dictates how you will respond to persons in such everyday exchanges. And this would further show that such an ethical stance is, after all, contingent, and not a necessary and primordial comportment of our mode of being towards others. My answer to this would be to suggest that our primordial ethical mode of being is indeed a basic or *prima facie* aspect of our existence as social beings but that it can be distorted by bad upbringing. The rude person is one whose basic goodness towards others has been overlain with discourtesy and blindness to the mystery of the other person as a result of experiences that have left them self-centred. In contrast, the courteous person, although they have had to learn the forms that courtesy should take in any given society, is giving expression to that primordial mode of being that marks us all off as ethical beings. But before we can accept this answer, we need an argument to suggest that our ethical mode of being is indeed a basic and ineliminable aspect of our existence.

To develop this argument we need to consider a further point that Levinas makes. He asks us to consider what it is to engage in dialogue. No one would deny that one of the most central and ineliminable features of human life is that people engage in conversations. Even people who do not have the physical wherewithal to speak create sign language so that they can communicate. What is striking about the millions of words that are spoken and written every day among people is that only some of them are of a functional or pragmatic nature. We do exchange information in order to get things done, but we also spend a lot of time speaking to each other in ways that have no practical use or functional outcome. The exchange about the weather with the man in the ticket booth was like that, and most of the conversation you had with your partner at that intimate candle-lit dinner would also have been like that, although this does raise the question of whether conversation aimed at shaping one's relationship with another can be thought of as "functional". Many of our conversations with others serve no purpose other than establishing, maintaining and deepening our relationships with them. But whether any given conversation is functional and goal-oriented or whether it is simply a social lubricant, one point remains clear: a conversation involves at least two parties. There is, at any given moment, a party who speaks and a party who listens. And being prepared to listen is always already an ethical stance of respect and openness to the other.

This very obvious point shows that the Nietzschean–existential stress on the self as a self-project is incomplete. In a Nietzschean–existential world there would only be speakers and no listeners. Having to listen would be seen as a threat to one's self-affirmation and will to power. But if dialogue is basic to human reality, if it is an aspect of our most primordial mode of being to be in communication with others, then that mode of being includes the stance of openness to, and respect for, others that is encapsulated in listening to them. Once again, there is no denying that human beings can be taught bad habits so that the art of listening respectfully is attenuated and has to be recovered with effort, but if human beings are fundamentally communicating beings, then the stance of listening is built into our very mode of being. This stance has an ethical quality and this quality is a primordial feature of the way we are, rather than a learnt and contingent feature of the characters of only those who are well brought up.

There is a further implication that can be drawn from this point. The ethics of duty relies on a conception of ethics as the product of rational thought. It affirms that an action is ethically good to the extent that it conforms to norms that can be rationally justified. But to be rational is to be impartial and objective and to abstract one's thinking from the concrete situation and relationships of which one is a part. It is, in this sense, to "dis-individuate" oneself. Levinas's point about dialogue is that we are never dis-individuated in this way. We are never abstract thinking entities without a context of relationships. We speak to each other and thereby address ourselves to one another and define ourselves as ethically engaged participants in dialogue with one another.

> The passage to the rational is not a dis-individuation precisely because it is language, that is, a response to the being who in a face speaks to the subject and tolerates only a personal response, that is, an ethical act.
>
> Emmanuel Levinas, *Totality and Infinity*, 219

The final point that I want to draw from Levinas is somewhat more technical. The Nietzschean–existential way of thinking about ethics puts the focus on the individual subject and hence is most readily articulated in the first-person voice. This tradition is concerned with what *I* should do and how *I* should live *my* life. It is my honesty in expressing my will to power that is at issue for Nietzsche and my authenticity in resisting the identity-imposing gaze of the other that is at issue for Sartre. In contrast to these approaches, Levinas stresses the way in which I am called to being ethical by being addressed by the other. It is not a matter of my affirming myself and saying "I", but a matter of responding to another who addresses me as "you". Primordially, I am a "you" for another rather than an "I" for myself. This point is an elaboration of the point about dialogue. Not only does dialogue entail a primordial stance of listening and respect for the other on my part, but it also entails being addressed by the other. This address by the other elicits my response and thus shapes the way that I express myself. I am a "you" even before I am an "I". The fundamental structure of my ethical stance is not that of a self-affirming stance against the world, but that of a response to the call of the other that is implicit in my being the "you" that they are addressing. Indeed, to put the point as radically as Levinas does himself, I owe my very existence as a self to the other.

This point is best explicated by imagining a scenario. I was recently standing waiting for the checkout at a greengrocer when an elderly gentleman came up to the queue carrying a lot of fruit and vegetables in his arms. He seemed not to want to use plastic bags. He was having trouble with his load and dropped a piece of fruit. Had he bent over to pick it up he would have dropped the rest of his selections. So I picked it up for him. This is not a very dramatic act of assistance and anyone would have done the same, but it nicely illustrates how an ethical act is often a response to an implicit call for help. The old man had not in fact asked for help but the very situation he was in called for it. I did not obey any command or any internalized norm; nor did I consciously seek to express my character in my action. I simply responded to a need. Levinas suggests that even where there is no explicit need inherent in a situation our ethical comportment towards others is structured in the way illustrated by this story. The other person, in their mystery and infinity, calls out to me, as it were, to respond to them in whatever way the situation calls for. If it is a conversation, I am called to listen. If they are in need, I am called to help. If they occupy a functional relationship to me, I am called upon to acknowledge them as a person through my courtesy. The whole of my social life is structured by such calls. They are part of the social environment in which my existence is shaped. So my mode of being is not just to be self-assertive despite the presence of others, it is to be responsive to others. I am what I am as a product not just of my own self-project but also of the calls upon me that others send out. The very infinity and mystery of the other is a call upon my responsiveness. As an ethical being I am what I am, not just as an expression of my self-affirmation, but also as a "you" that others address from out of their needs and vulnerabilities. I am made not only by my self-project but also by the call upon me that others send out to me. (Perhaps this is the reason for the continuing appeal of the image of morality as a set of commands issued by God. The Ten Commandments are a call upon our ethical response issued by that being whom we take to be the ultimate Other and to whose mystery and infinity we respond ethically so as to define ourselves as ethical.)

> In expression the being that imposes itself does not limit but promotes my freedom, by arousing my goodness.
>
> Emmanuel Levinas, *Totality and Infinity*, 200

The consequences of these arguments are very profound for Levinas. They show that the primacy of the self that was assumed by the Nietzschean–existential tradition is misplaced. Not only is the other not just an object for my apprehension or a threat to my authenticity, but they are a call upon me that constitutes my identity through my accepting that call and taking responsibility for it. Without the call that emanates from the other, I would not be who I am. So the reality of the other is more fundamental than my own. I come into being through my response to the other. Of course, I do not mean by this that my physical existence as a biological being is brought into being in this way. Rather, I mean that my existence as a self-project and as an openness to others is constituted by the call of the other upon me. We could illustrate this by considering a very young infant responding to the call of its mother. While it is a biological being with needs that cause it to seek its mother's nurture, it is that nurture that awakens in it those first glimmers of human response such as a smile and its first words. It is in response to its care-givers that it comes to its own being as a self-project. Its being as openness to others is therefore more basic than its project of self-affirmation. It is from the very first an ethical being. I am always already the kind of being that can respond to the caring call of the other.

And it is not just the caring of the other to which I respond. As I grow older I also come to respond to the vulnerability of the other. Whereas my own vulnerability, finitude and mortality are conditions that I tend to ignore as I go through life believing that misfortune will not happen to me, the vulnerability of others, especially those whom I love, is constantly before me. It is this that elicits in me my feeling of responsibility for them and constitutes me as an ethical being in relation to them.

Rather than defining our ethical selves just as expressions of a universal rationality encapsulated in the autonomy of individuals, as the Kantian tradition does, for Levinas the response that defines us as ethically good arises from the call of others. This call constitutes me as responsible for them. Responsibility in this sense is a primordial, ethical comportment towards others that is an aspect of our mode of being as social and communicating animals. Levinas draws further and very ethically demanding conclusions from this notion of responsibility but I do not want to explore his thought further in this direction. The conclusion that I want to draw from these suggestions is that being ethical in the sense of having a respectful and responsive stance towards others is indeed a primordial aspect of our mode of being as human beings. We are always already ethical. Our virtuous character is an expression of this mode of being arising from the fortunate but contingent upbringing that we may have received and from the efforts of self-making that we will have engaged in.

Levinas deepens Hume's theory by suggesting that our response to others is not just a feeling or sentiment that most human beings contingently express, but part of the very structure of our being: a structure without which we could not be who we are. So, if Nietzsche's challenge to us is that we should become who we are, Levinas's theory suggests that this implies that our responsibility for others would be central to this task. Our very ethical identity is called into being by the call of others. Virtue then becomes not just a habit ingrained in our characters by our upbringing, but a fundamental aspect of our mode of being as human beings. Without any appeal to God or to metaphysics (although he was a devout Jew and also wrote on religious themes), Levinas creates an image of human existence and of moral psychology in which caring about others is as primordial an aspect of our mode of being as is our self-project. Our identity – our being who we are – is as bound up with our ethical response to others as it is with our striving for self-realization. Virtue is fundamental to our existence. Rather than the disengagement from the world that the Stoics and others taught, responsiveness to, and responsibility for, the world and for others are the hallmarks of virtue.

It would appear then that the point of being virtuous is twofold. Aristotle and the ancients focused on the fulfilment of the self as the inherent goal of being virtuous, Aquinas stressed personal salvation, and Nietzsche uncovered the self-affirmation and self-realization that lie at the heart of our motivations. These approaches highlight our being as self-project. In contrast, Hume highlighted the concern for others that is among our motivating passions, whereas Levinas detected responsiveness to, and responsibility for, others in the very mode of our being. These thinkers highlight our being as caring-about-others. I would argue that the point of being virtuous is to give equal expression to these two aspects of our being. If I may use Aristotle's teleological framework, I would conclude that the inherent goal of being virtuous is not only to achieve *eudaimoniā* for ourselves, but also to fulfil ourselves as social and interpersonal beings concerned for the well-being of others.

Summary and conclusion

This chapter continues our survey of the history of the idea of virtue but also begins to develop an argument about some of the theoretical tenets of virtue theory: that ethics is not a transcendent but a worldly matter; that the emotions are more important than reason in our ethical lives; and that our relationships to others are not made ethical by moral norms and principles but are ethical from the very first. More specifically, it argues the following points:

- According to Hume, it is not possible to derive moral principles from reason alone.
- Sympathy is an important interpersonal emotion and a possible basis for a virtuous stance towards others.
- Nietzsche's concept of will to power is important for understanding the importance of self-realization as a motivator towards virtue.
- Nietzsche's distinction between slave morality and master morality introduces the idea that differing moral outlooks and the virtues that they promote can coexist and that some virtues are more admirable than others, depending on the outlook that one has.
- The Nietzschean–existential conception of human beings as self-affirming and free individuals – which is a development of the Enlightenment moral theory that underpins much of the ethics of duty – makes it difficult to see how concern for others can be a basic ethical stance in human lives.
- Levinas argues that, because we cannot assimilate others into our own view of the world, our most primordial mode of being is already ethical. We are constituted by others as responsible for them.

This chapter has contributed to two of the tasks of moral theory that I identified in the Introduction: understanding what morality is and showing what place the norms we live by have in our lives. Morality, I can now suggest, is the set of norms that gives form to our fundamentally ethical stance towards others. Its place in our lives is not that of an external set of rules or principles to which we must be obedient, but that of an internalized form given to our self-project and our primordial concern for others. Virtue is not just that set of character traits that are required of us or applauded by others. It is the structure that others give to us in so far as we respond to their call upon us. It is our way of being ethical. Like Hume's sympathy, it is a prerequisite for being moral in that it provides the motivational basis for our doing our duty. But unlike Hume's sympathy, it is not a feeling that we may or may not have depending on our upbringing or genetic makeup, but a mode of our very being. These theoretical explorations explain why reasons internalism (as explained in Ch. 1, "The nature of norms", §VII) is important to virtue ethics. Hume's notion of sympathy was an early attempt to explain how it was that ethical concern for the other needed to be part of the internal motivations of virtuous agents, whereas Levinas's analysis explains how such motivations are part of the very structure of our being. Without such accounts we would have no reason to be virtuous except obedience to external command.

What I have not yet done in my exposition is to indicate what virtues we should prescribe and why (although we have seen some suggestions on this matter from Nietzsche – suggestions that we may not want to agree with.) In order to broach this question we shall have to explore the concept of justice and what it demands from us. This is one of the tasks of Chapter 4.

four

Reconciling virtue and justice

Introduction

I concluded Chapter 3 with the suggestion that the point of ethics was not only to achieve self-fulfilment and self-realization (which are possible interpretations of Aristotle's notion of *eudaimoniā* as well as of Nietzsche's will to power) but also to fulfil our primordial mode of being as social beings who care about, and are responsible for, others. This suggestion certainly enhances the Aristotelian framework of virtue ethics in that it embraces concern for others more fully than Aristotle had done himself, but it still confines itself to those others with whom I have direct and friendly contact. Levinas had spoken of the face-to-face relationship, and Aristotle's account of *philia*, which is often translated as "friendship", also stays within this ambit. It describes the nature and bases of those relationships that are available to people in communities in which everyone enjoys some face-to-face relations with others: relations ranging from those of mutual usefulness and pleasure, to those of close friendship based on character.

Modern societies pose a different problem. In nation-states and other large and impersonal societies social norms cannot be based on ethical face-to-face relationships between people. They must be based on principles that everyone can accept on the basis of a public discourse adhering to standards of impartiality, objectivity and rationality. Rather than adhering to the norms of *philia* or love and caring between individuals as shaped by tradition, they must adhere to the norms of justice and of morality as articulated in terms that can be universalized. Some philosophers suggest that the objective and principle-based discourse of duty ethics is relevant to public policy and criminal law, whereas virtue ethics is more important to the ethical lives of individuals and communities. Following the inspiration of Aristotle, they say that virtue ethics is about how we might individually achieve *eudaimoniā*, albeit as enhanced by relationships of *philia* with particular others, whereas morality and the law articulate those norms that are necessary for general social harmony. In this broader context, virtue is important only in so far as it helps people to obey the law and do their duty. In this chapter I shall argue that virtue ethics is primary and can be extended from the sphere of personal fulfilment and interpersonal relationships to that of public and civic life.

The expanding circle

One way in which we might extend our thinking from the individual and interpersonal level where virtue is constitutive of *eudaimoniā* to the more impersonal social level is to use and extend Aristotle's conception of *philia*. Aristotle was trying to explain how it is that we can get on with other people and why they are important in our lives even when it is our own *eudaimoniā* that we are implicitly seeking. Some people are of use to us, others give us pleasure of one kind or another and a select few are our friends. Friendships in their turn are based on a mutual recognition on the part of the friends of their virtue and goodness of character. We enjoy the company of our friends because they are a reflection of our own virtue and thereby reinforce our sense of fulfilment. In these ways we both need and enjoy sociability with others, and our ethical concern is extended towards those others. If we are ethically good, we do good things for the sake of our friends. Accordingly, our ethical concern widens beyond merely our own *eudaimoniā* in order to embrace the well-being of some others.

Some philosophers suggest that our concern for others who are strangers to us, and our concern for social justice, can be accounted for as a further extension of these bonds of sociability. For example, we form bonds with all those people who share a common identity with us, whether that identity is based on religion, nationality, ethnicity, neighbourhood, gender or common history. And these various identity-conferring memberships can overlap in a variety of ways as well. We are members of communities of various kinds and of varying levels of importance to us. The shared outlooks inherent in these communities provide a basis for mutual caring and hence extend the scope of our ethical concerns. Within communities, it is virtuous to care about our fellows in those communities.

Carol Gilligan's ethics of caring, which I discussed in Chapter 1, is also relevant here. Although we "naturally" care about those who are close to us because, for example, they are members of our families, it is also virtuous to care about those for whom we have professional responsibilities, for example, as teachers or as nurses. Indeed, the circle of those about whom it is virtuous to care need not be confined just to these two spheres. You are the more virtuous the wider the circle of those about whom you care. You should care about the starving in the third world and about the victims of war and natural disaster. Even when you have nothing in common with those people or share no identity-forming community memberships with them, they are human beings and, as such, should elicit your care and concern. All those who share a common humanity should be the objects of our care. Indeed, your caring about others could extend even beyond the human species. Any being that can suffer, whether an intelligent ape or a chicken, should elicit your concern. Even if the latter form of caring is not yet widespread in human communities, the expanding circle of ethical caring will and should embrace it in due course.

The theoretical foundations for these suggestions as to how the ethical pursuit of *eudaimoniā* might extend to others in ever wider circles of concern might be found in Hume's notion of an inherent feeling of sympathy of human beings or in Levinas's conception of our being open to the call of the other in their infinite mystery. It is also suggested by the Christian conception of love for all humankind to which we are enjoined by God's love for us.

But there is a problem. By modelling our concern for others-in-general on our concern, caring or love for those particular others with whom we have face-to-face relationships, these theories misunderstand the nature of the ethical stance that is in question. It is not caring, love, concern, sympathy, benevolence nor any form of *philia* that is at issue in this broader context; it is justice. Modern societies are not communities in the sense of groupings bound by widening forms of *philia*. They are pluralistic aggregations bound by general norms backed by the force of law. These norms are the product of public debate that is ideally structured by the norms of justice and impartiality rather than feelings of caring and sympathy. The discourse of liberal, pluralist politics prescinds from relations of *philia* precisely because it requires a negotiable public realm in which everyone is subject to law irrespective of bonds of love, membership of communities or relationships of caring. In this discourse, the moral status of an individual does not depend on the community of which she is a member or on the relationships she enjoys with others. It depends on her having rights before the law: rights that should be available equally to everyone within that political society. It is definitive of justice that everyone should enjoy equality before the law, obtain what is theirs by right, and be treated in accordance with their deserts.

How can virtue theory take us from the discourse of *philia*, caring, love and benevolence, to a discourse of justice, equality and impartiality if the latter is not to be seen as an extension of the former? Are these discourses as distinct and unbridgeable as I suggested in Chapter 1? In order to answer these questions I propose to explore a thesis put forward by Paul Ricoeur (1913–2005) who is a leading thinker in the hermeneutic tradition.

Hermeneutics: Paul Ricoeur

Before we explore Ricoeur's view we need to give Aristotle a hermeneutic reading. In the hermeneutic tradition, to understand a phenomenon is to interpret it in the light of a larger "whole" of which one already has some degree of understanding and, at the same time, to contribute to the understanding of that whole by explicating the phenomenon that one is trying to understand. Rather than appeal to causal hypotheses or to metaphysical or epistemological doctrines that would provide a secure foundation for theory, hermeneutics appeals to the meaning-giving context in which a phenomenon occurs and to the implicit "pre-understanding" that enquirers bring to the enquiry in order to make the phenomenon being studied intelligible. In this way, we might suggest that our understanding of *eudaimoniā* can be hermeneutical in form. Our understanding of ourselves as persons and as beings directed on the goal of happiness is a framework that we cannot but have for understanding our lives, our desires, attitudes, projects and beliefs. We understand our lives in the light of a holistic and overarching conception: namely, the Aristotelian theory that the goal or *telos* of a human life is *eudaimoniā* achieved through rational action. From this it follows that a good human being is one who pursues *eudaimoniā* well by exercising all of the functions of their mode of being (or parts of the soul). Understanding all this as a hermeneutic postulate means that we do not have to posit a metaphysical theory about human nature to ground the *telos* of *eudaimoniā* (and we thereby escape Hume's criticisms of such theories). Rather, we make sense of the wide variety of human phenomena by seeing them as so many expressions of this rational quest for happiness. If we are studying the customs of a foreign people we would not be able to make sense of anything they were doing unless we assumed that their primordial purpose was to achieve *eudaimoniā*. We might need to define what we meant by that, but their practices would be completely unintelligible to us unless we used some such framework for understanding them. In this way, we interpret Aristotle as offering us not a metaphysical theory about the rational souls of human beings that claims that all human beings are so structured as to pursue *eudaimoniā* and that a good human being is one who does this well, but a framework for understanding human beings and what they do: a framework that begins with the premise that, fundamentally, all human beings pursue *eudaimoniā*. It is in the light of this premise that we can then go on to make sense of the many and varied ways in which people live and also to evaluate what they do as being conducive or not to that postulated goal.

Apart from avoiding the need for metaphysical theories, a further benefit of the hermeneutic method is that it leaves us free to posit a "whole" for interpreting the parts in the light of what may prove most useful in aiding understanding. Our postulate can be purely pragmatic. Whatever helps us make sense of human events and actions is a valid postulation. In this way, for example, we can see Nietzsche's concept of will to power as a hermeneutic postulate for understanding human life, albeit one that we found unsatisfactory on its own. It is legitimate, therefore, to consider alternative or expanded postulates as to what the *telos* of human existence might be. We can use the teleological framework of Aristotle's ethical theory and put into the position occupied by *eudaimoniā* a fuller concept that will allow us to render human life and individual effort more intelligible than Aristotle's own concept does.

This is what Ricoeur does in his book *Oneself as Another*. Ricoeur suggests that the *telos* of human existence can be articulated as an "ethical aim": to live well, with and for others, in just institutions. By the simple expedient of building both *philia* and the political goals of justice into the *telos* of human existence along with *eudaimoniā*, Ricoeur obviates the need to derive sociability and political goals from the *telos* of a merely personal and individual fulfilment. The concept of *eudaimoniā*, because its logical grammar is that of the hermeneutic "whole" through which our lives are made intelligible, can accommodate whatever theoreticians would postulate as basic in the rational concerns of human beings. The test for the adequacy of such a postulate is that it accords with our intuitive "pre-understanding" and that it serves to make human life intelligible. And so, rather than conceive of our human *telos* as individual happiness or fulfilment, Ricoeur suggests that it also includes our goal of forming interpersonal relationships with particular others, and our inclination towards living in societies marked by the central features of justice: features such as equality before the law, being treated according to one's deserts, and a fair distribution of social goods. In this way, a desire for personal fulfilment, a disposition to form loving bonds with others, and a sense of fairness are seen as equally primordial in human existence. Human life cannot be understood as a rational whole unless we acknowledge this threefold aim. Moreover, we can articulate what it is for a human being to be good or virtuous by seeing how well that human being achieves the aims of self-fulfilment, forms benevolent relationships with particular others and acts as a political agent with a view to securing justice for all.

But Ricoeur's analysis is not only hermeneutic. It is not only an attempt to render human life and ethical values intelligible. It is also existential. It is an attempt to understand the dynamic nature of the self and of subjectivity in terms of what it is seeking. If virtue ethics asks "What should I be?" more often than "What should I do?", then it must engage with the question of how I form my ethical identity. The self seeks to forge its own identity and respond to the call of others in the context of the threefold aim that Ricoeur has postulated. My existence as self-project and as caring-about-others is realized and fulfilled in the way in which I seek to live well, with and for others, in just institutions. Ricoeur uses the concept of "attestation" to articulate this idea. My self attests to itself and creates its own identity by the stances it takes in relation to the ethical aim as pursued with others in society. The identity of the self is not just a product of the processes of socialization that shape it but also of the attestation of that self in relation to particular others and to society. I am shaped by others but I also affirm myself in relation to them. It is the way in which the self attests to its *telos* and expresses its threefold ethical aim in the world that constitutes its identity and its virtue. In this way Ricoeur is expressing the Nietzschean–existential idea of the self as a product of its self-affirmation or attestation, but is also acknowledging the importance of others and of society as a structuring of that attestation. This enlarges the scope and meaning of ethics so that it embraces both my self-project and my caring-about-others.

Ricoeur also seems to embrace Nietzsche's idea that the self is not unitary. Without using Nietzsche's notion of a multitude of wills contesting within us for dominance, Ricoeur does speak of our attesting to ourselves in a variety of forms. In one context I am an individual seeking my own fulfilment, in another context I am a husband acting for the sake of my wife. In one context I am a political agent acting on behalf of the common good without regard for my own particular interests, in another I am a religious believer affirming a faith and a tradition possibly at variance with the dominant beliefs of my society. Whether these varying roles or identities can be integrated is not as important as that they be honoured. My virtue consists in being faithful to all of them.

> I propose to establish, without concerning myself about Aristotelian or Kantian orthodoxy, although not without paying close attention to the founding texts of these two traditions: (1) the primacy of ethics over morality, (2) the necessity for the ethical aim to pass through the sieve of the norm, and (3) the legitimacy of recourse by the norm to the aim whenever the norm leads to impasses in practice.   Paul Ricoeur, *Oneself as Another*, 170

Ricoeur also distinguishes the *ethical* concerns of human existence (which are broadly those theorized by Aristotle) from *moral* concerns. The former focus on the goal of living well as a fulfilment of our threefold ethical aim, whereas the latter focus on the norms and prohibitions in accordance with which we are obliged to live within society. Further, beyond ethical and moral concerns, Ricoeur also recognizes a political level of existence. What is at issue at each of these three levels is the form that our identity takes when we express our ethical aim at these levels.

Given that our ethical aim is itself tripartite, Ricoeur's position, when fully elaborated, may be schematically represented as in Table 2.

Table 2 Ricoeur's ethical aim

The ethical aim	Expression in ethical (teleological) discourse	Expression in moral (deontological) discourse	Expression in political discourse
The desire to live well	Self-esteem	Autonomy giving rise to self-respect	Conviction and action
The desire to live well with and for others	Solicitude and reciprocity	The Golden Rule	Critical solicitude
The desire to live well in just institutions	A sense of common purpose	Formal principles of justice	Pluralist liberal politics

The ethical aim

The first column of Table 2 articulates the ethical aim that Ricoeur posits as the internal fulfilment of human existence, and splits it into three levels. It suggests that the individual pursuit of *eudaimoniā*, the social and community-based pursuit of *philia*, and the social and political pursuit of justice are equiprimordial goals inherent in human life. We cannot make sense of what people do unless we assume that these goals together constitute the point of human existence. The column headings are the three forms of articulation that the ethical aim receives as people are defined in their social contexts and attest to their identities in three distinguishable discourses: the discourse of ethics that articulates the pursuit of personal fulfilment; the discourse of morality that articulates our duties; and the discourse of political debate and the making of law and public policy that articulates our pursuit of social harmony.

Self-esteem

The second column shows how the ethical aim is expressed in the ethical life of individuals and in the identities that they form in the ethical dimension of their lives. So, individual success in the enterprise of living well comes to expression in our ethical lives as a feeling of self-esteem. We feel good about ourselves in so far as we live virtuously and achieve the kind of self-fulfilment that Aristotle had highlighted as constitutive of *eudaimoniā*.

Solicitude and reciprocity

In the second row Ricoeur explicates the interpersonal aspects of the ethical aim with reference to Aristotle's account of friendship. Our desire to live well with and for others is articulated as solicitude for particular others with whom I have a relationship of *philia*. We act for the sake of their good. Moreover, my friends are solicitous for me in so far as they are my friends. Given the symmetrical nature of friendship, therefore, my reaching out to others both constitutes me as a friend and makes me the object of the reciprocal concern of my friends. This analysis extends to spouses and other intimate life-partners as well. The idea is that my concern for myself – my self-project – becomes enlarged by my existence within my family, web of friendships and community. In this context my virtues as a friend – virtues such as loyalty and benevolence – become part of my identity. I am no longer wrapped up in myself. I attest to, and fulfil, this new form of myself by exercising the virtues of friendship. A key point for Ricoeur, however, is that this analysis applies to particular others who are known to me in their uniqueness and particularity.

A sense of common purpose

This perspective does not apply so strongly to the third row in the second column. This box refers to the social level of our existence and suggests that people see their fellows in a community as engaged on a common enterprise of living well. To be a member of a community might not involve sharing close or friendly relationships with all other members, but it does involve sharing an outlook on life and a sense of purpose. Members of a religious denomination see themselves as engaged in a shared spiritual quest. Members and supporters of particular political parties share an ideology. People of the same race, especially when that race has been exploited, oppressed or abused, share a common identity-forming history. Employees in organizations share in a common enterprise. And members of the same nation often see themselves as sharing a national destiny. To be virtuous in the context of these identity-forming memberships involves such qualities of character as patriotism, pride in one's community, commitment and piety. We exercise such virtues by acknowledging the common purposes of our lives and attesting to our identity as members of such communities. Philosophers who call themselves "communitarians" argue that virtues take on their meaning and significance in the context of the shared purposes and values of particular communities in this way.

What is striking about our identity as it is shaped at this level of our ethical aim is that we are less important as unique individuals. It is our membership of the relevant community that defines who we are and what it is for us to be good. Our ethical aim is no longer centred upon ourselves, but begins to constitute us as having a role among others. There may be traditional hierarchies, or there may be democratic processes for selecting leaders, but everyone has status in so far as they fill a role. We gain self-esteem to the extent that we are not submerged into an anonymous mass, but we enjoy no priority over others that is not sanctioned by the group. We have an identity and a status, but it is not based on our own individuality. As members of our communities it is our fulfilment of the roles of membership and our adherence to the traditions and beliefs of the community that constitute our virtue. Under the authority of tradition we adhere to the norms that apply impartially to our roles.

The virtue of solidarity, which is central to this mode of being, involves some effacement of the self, but also promises an enhancement of the self that comes from membership of the community and identification with its traditions. One fulfils oneself by taking pride in one's community and adhering to its common purposes. The norms and traditions of the community are internalized as an expression of both one's self-project and one's caring-about-others. Accordingly, one's commitment to the values and norms of one's community and traditions will take on a high degree of practical necessity. One will feel strongly bound by those norms and standards since one's very identity as a member of the community is at stake. Moreover, there will be customs and virtues that are strongly expressive of the tradition. In some communities, for example, extreme modesty and various forms of subservience will be virtuous for women whereas men are expected to be aggressively protective of their women. Both men and women in those communities will feel that it is strongly obligatory to adhere to those standards.

Although *philia* is marked by reciprocity, it still situates the self as being at the centre of interpersonal relationships. My concern for others emanates from a self that continues to hold a privileged position as the one who cares. My concern for others grounds my self-esteem because it gives form to my virtue of benevolence and loyalty. *Philia* remains self-centred although not selfish. The self that finds itself within a web of interpersonal relationships still gives preference if not to itself then to those with whom it enjoys relationships of *philia*. We want to see our children succeed. We want to see our friends prosper. These valid concerns make us partial. We privilege those who are close to us because our own interests are bound up with theirs. Similarly, living in communities leads us to privilege our fellow religionists, our work colleagues, our co-nationals and so forth. Although our focus upon ourselves and those close to us is reducing, our position is still partial and based on a shared sense of purpose. Even if we regard the "community" of which we are a member and with which we identify as humanity itself so as to extend the obligations and standards of membership to the whole of the human family, we will still be using ourselves as a benchmark for what that means. This is a fine and virtuous stance and one that can motivate humanitarian aid around the world, but it is still one that emanates from caring and generosity: virtues that emanate from the fullness of the self. We are on the way to justice but we are not there yet. We are still living an ethical life as opposed to a moral one.

Autonomy giving rise to self-respect

The third column of the table is explicated by Ricoeur in broadly Kantian terms. It is here that the self is conceived as a rational agent whose self-respect is grounded in the degree to which mere inclinations can be overcome in order to act well. Ricoeur does not endorse Kant's exclusive stress on reason but he does acknowledge that moral thinking requires a degree of objectivity about ourselves and an ability to transcend our desires and inclinations. We need to acknowledge the demands upon us that arise from others and from society. It is in this that our autonomy consists. But from Ricoeur's hermeneutic perspective this autonomy is seen as a fulfilment of our aim towards living well rather than as a metaphysical postulation, as it was for Kant. In order to make sense of our lives in the context of modernity we need to see it as inherent in us to want to achieve autonomy in the sense of self-control and the ability to direct our lives rationally, rather than being subject to whims, desires, bonds of affection, or even community traditions. Our self-respect would seem to depend on it.

The Golden Rule

When Ricoeur considers the "with and for others" qualification of living well within the discourse of morality, he is led to the Golden Rule: "Do unto others as you would have them do unto you". This is a more adequate articulation of our stance towards others than Kant's categorical imperative because it stresses reciprocity and mutuality without situating one's self at the centre of moral concerns. One sees oneself as another and the other as a self. One acknowledges that the other can be an autonomous agent and that one can oneself be the passive recipient of the actions of another. It asks us to consider ourselves as others might see us and to apply the same standard to others as we want them to apply to us. This involves seeing ourselves more objectively and not just in the light of our own interests. We come to see ourselves as a node in a system of formal relationships in which each (including ourselves) is given their due. This involves a shift of discourses from the ethical discourse of securing my happiness, the interests of those close to me, and the aspirations of my communities, to a moral discourse that involves respecting the rights of others, the dignity of the individual and what is due to people in fairness and in law. One adopts a new stance and attests to a new identity. This stance is not a further development of the ethical stance described in the second column, but a new form of identity with a new set of virtues.

Formal principles of justice

This becomes clear as we explore the third row in the third column. The identity to which I attest in pursuing my goal of living well in just institutions and the identity that I ascribe to others in this context is that of an "each". If the central rubric of this level of thinking is "to each according to justice" then both the other and I are such an "each". Impartial thinking demands that I see myself as another in a sphere of distribution, retribution and other social arrangements in which my needs or desires are not privileged over that of any other person. Nor may the needs and desires of those whom I love or with whom I share a common purpose be given any privilege in this sphere. Everyone is an impersonal "each": a node in a system of social distribution and institutional arrangements in which the moral and legal equality of each is to be guaranteed. Ricoeur insists that as we move from the sphere of *philia* or sociability to the sphere of justice, a qualitative change takes place in the way that the self conceives of itself and of others. The continuity between the sphere of *philia* and that of justice is not grounded in the latter's being an extension of *philia*. Rather, it is grounded in the ethical aim, which, at the level of society, is a pursuit of equality articulated in institutions rather than in relationships. The virtue of justice is therefore understood as the virtue of giving each his or her due rather than as loyalty or fidelity to friends, or as solidarity with communities. The perspective of justice constitutes the self as neutral and impersonal and as capable of seeing all others as true equals in moral and social standing.

Accordingly, the virtue of justice involves a different stance or attestation of the self from the virtues of family, friendship, and community. The just person is one who does not place himself, his loved ones or his community colleagues at the centre of his concerns but rather sees himself and others impartially as so many equal units in a field of justice. This requires a stance of objectivity about oneself and others. Objectivity here means letting go of one's own individual perspective and even the perspective of one's community and its traditional beliefs, and adopting the stance of an impartial participant. Imagine a child that has hurt itself. It cries. Its mother says to it, "Please don't cry, Matilda. Mummy has a headache and your crying is making it worse." Matilda would have to have achieved some level of maturity in order to be able to respond to this appropriately. If she is very young she will not be able to do this. She will not be able to take the needs of her mother into account. She will be totally preoccupied with her own distress. She is not able to be objective. Were she more mature she might be able to balance her concern for her mother with her concern for her own problem and meet her mother's need. But this requires her to be virtuous. Adopting the stance of justice involves this kind of move from self-preoccupation to objectivity. It is a move to autonomy. At the social level if involves seeing oneself as no more important than anyone else.

The essence of the virtue of justice then is to stop seeing oneself as the centre of the world and to attest to oneself as one among many. It is to stop taking oneself to be an exception or to be more important than anyone else. It is even to stop being the centre of a circle of *philia*, or care and concern, no matter how widely that circle is expanding. The just person is not the centre of anything. She is merely one among many, enjoying equal status with the many and claiming no privilege for herself. She is an "each". As Ricoeur puts it in the title of his book, one sees oneself as another. To attest to this form of ethical identity is virtue indeed.

Ricoeur refers to the political philosopher John Rawls when he explicates how our desire to live well in just institutions is expressed through formal principles of justice. The principles that Rawls puts forward are that there must be a maximum amount of freedom consistent with social order (with the consequence that there will be disparities of wealth), that social goods must be distributed in such a way that even the poorest benefit from the increases in wealth that the rich enjoy, and that all positions of social power must be accessible to everyone. Although it is not the purpose of this book to explore such principles in full, it is worth noting that the strategy by which Rawls arrives at them instantiate the virtue of justice as I have just explained it. Rawls draws an imaginary scenario in which representatives of the community are to decide upon the institutions and principles of a just society from behind a "veil of ignorance". This means that these representatives do not know what position they will have in the new society or what their status will be in it. They may be poor or rich, black or white, male or female, disabled or fully abled and so on. From behind such a veil a representative will only agree to arrangements that will be of some benefit to the least privileged in society, given that they might themselves belong to this category. Accordingly, any arrangement that would be agreed to in such a scenario will be just. But this scenario could be said to embrace the conditions of objectivity and impartiality that I explained above. If you do not know where you will end up in the new society, then you will adopt the position of anyone at all in that society rather than your own actual position. The veil of ignorance prevents you from using the advantage you have been given by knowing more about your own case and about your own powers and privileges. Accordingly, parties to the original contract are effectively equals. This is precisely the virtuous stance of objectivity and impartiality that defines the self of the just person. It involves regarding everyone, including oneself, as of equal status.

However, Ricoeur does not agree that Rawls's formal principles are as purely procedural and abstract as Rawls himself would assert. In so far as they are principles of justice that are motivated by our ethical aim, they will articulate our substantial conceptions of what a good life is as well as our ideals of a good society. For some this might mean state provision of basic necessities whereas for others it will mean the operation of a free market. For others again it might mean theocracy. These differing conceptions will be expressive of differing conceptions of what it is to live well with and for others in just institutions: that is, differing and often irreconcilable conceptions of virtue and of morality. These conceptions often arise from the community traditions in which a particular individual is formed. We bring our ethical ideals with us as we move into the realm of morality and justice. The second and third columns of Table 2 are not separated from each other. According to Ricoeur, a merely formal or abstract conception of justice will fail to express our substantive ethical aims.

Pluralist liberal policies

The fact that there can be disagreement on substantive conceptions of the good in the political sphere creates the need for a further level of reconciliation. This takes us to the final column of our table and initially to the third row. Political discourse in a liberal society will be pluralist and ongoing. Rather than reconciling differing points of view through a commonality based on *philia* or community, Ricoeur recognizes that the grounding of individual and community convictions in myth, metaphysics and tradition leads to tragic dilemmas for individuals as they seek to negotiate competing norms, and irreconcilable differences between people and communities as they articulate their ethical aim through conflicting conceptions of goodness and justice. It is for this reason that political and moral debate must transcend individual convictions, bonds of *philia* and community commitments and become truly pluralist. Convictions and bonds that are not transcended in this way can only be advanced by force. In order to establish a polity of shared power, political discourse must respect the plurality of views and seek to create policy that is acceptable to all. If this were a continuation of the bonds of community, the pluralist project would fail and domination by the most powerful community would ensue. Nevertheless, the convictions of individuals and communities must be allowed to exist in order for those individuals and communities to attain *eudaimoniā* in whatever form those convictions might indicate. People of secular conviction might engage in "the pursuit of happiness" whereas those of religious conviction might pursue eternal salvation. These varying pursuits will involve differing moral convictions – for example, on sexual mores – and individuals and communities will be inclined to think that those who differ from themselves in such convictions are wrong or evil. If these matters pertain to law and public policy – as abortion does, for example – debate on these issues may well be marked by acrimony and an unwillingness to reach compromise. Accordingly, political debate must be conducted at a level that transcends these convictions. What virtues does this necessity call for?

Critical solitude

Ricoeur argues that political debate must be marked by "critical solicitude". What this means is that there must be concern and respect for others even as all participants subject their own views and those of others to critical reason. Once again the aim of living well *with and for others* is expressed in a reciprocity of respect in which one's self is seen as another rather than as a privileged bearer of convictions that must be defended against others or imposed on them. One's own convictions are valid expressions of one's own ethical aim. However, as one moves from the personal through the interpersonal to the social, one moves also from a reflective and interpersonal form of private discourse to a public and non-personal discourse. One's own convictions and one's family and community bonds are here transcended and one takes on the identity of a political agent. Here the appropriate virtues are tolerance of diversity, and willingness to subject all views to critical scrutiny, including one's own. One must test one's convictions against social norms and subject them to the discipline of debate.

Conviction and action

One does not, however, lose one's commitment to one's own convictions as one respects the convictions of others and advocates those laws and policies that would allow others to practise the ways of life dear to them. The unity and rational coherence of this position is established by its being an expression of our desire to live well with and for others in just institutions rather than of our conviction that our own way of life is the only rational or morally correct one. It is the expression of our virtue of justice: of our stance of objectivity. It is not because one cares about those others necessarily (although one might). After all, how could you extend *philia* to people whose practices are strange to your eyes? Can you love those who perform clitorectomies on their infant daughters? For those who cannot, virtue suggests that they need the objectivity that would ground tolerance and the willingness to engage in rational debate that both expresses one's own convictions and also respects the other's difference. We must always remember that our own practices look as bizarre to others as theirs look to us. Reciprocity here may not take the form of friendship or care, but it must still adhere to the morality of the Golden Rule and to the political values of tolerance and rational debate.

In a world of differing conceptions of what it is to live well and of various moral convictions we would seem to be torn between a blind adherence to the convictions with which we have been brought up or a fluid tolerance of the convictions and practices of others that would amount to little more than cultural relativism. The only authentic and thus virtuous stance in this context is to engage in critical reflection and social debate. Our own views and the views of others must measure up to the standards of rational discussion: that is, they must be understandable by anyone who is prepared to give them rational consideration rather than being based on arcane or metaphysical doctrines that are immune to rational scrutiny. But these debates and reflections never seem to achieve resolution. No one worldview ever meets with universal agreement. No matter what the claims to universality of various moral and religious traditions, difference and pluralism continue to obtain. Accordingly, individuals of virtue will not consider their own convictions to be absolute. Intellectual virtue will include a sense of humility and respect for difference. The alternative is dogmatism and fanaticism.

> A liberal pluralist society will organize itself around the principle of maximum feasible accommodation of diverse legitimate ways of life, limited only by the minimum requirements of civic duty. This principle expresses (and requires) the practice of tolerance – the conscientious reluctance to act in ways that impede others from living in accordance with their various conceptions of what gives life meaning and worth. Tolerance is the virtue sustaining the social practices and political institutions that make expressive liberty possible. William A. Galston, *Liberal Pluralism*, 119

And yet to live well we must act. We must put our convictions – once they have been tested in critical solicitude and political debate – into effect. We know that we may be wrong and that our ethical aim may be frustrated, but this is an inevitable function of our finitude and fallibility. It is the tragic dimension of even a rational life. We cannot deduce our actions and policies from putatively universal principles, but must exercise judgement as best we can. We have to trust that our own decisions are the right ones although no one can assure us of this, and we have to trust others to also act in good faith, at least until there is clear evidence that they are not doing so. The virtuous way of acting upon one's convictions is with humility and tolerance. In large and impersonal political states, selves express themselves as citizens. The identity to which we attest at this level of our existence is that of the citizen. The virtues of such citizens include the pursuit of justice, trust in others and the tolerance of difference. Interpersonal caring may enrich these virtues but it cannot ground them or be demanded by them. And theoretical reason may not be able to reconcile them.

Ricoeur builds a conceptual structure in which an Aristotelian conception of virtue is basic. Given the expanded ethical aim of living well with and for others in just institutions, we can define those traits that will be virtues in the domains of our own existence, of our relationships with others and our communities, and of citizenship. This account will also explain why, in these three domains, we give ourselves the moral norms that we do. And it explains how, when there is contestation over these norms, it is our virtues that must arbitrate.

Summary and conclusion

In this chapter I have argued for the following points:

- It is not adequate to account for our responsibilities towards others by extending Aristotle's conception of friendship to all others, or by expanding the circle of those we care about. In so far as such responsibilities are a matter of justice, they must be thought of differently.
- Using Ricoeur's hermeneutic approach we can fill out Aristotle's notion of the inherent goal of human striving by positing an ethical aim that consists in living well with and for others in just institutions. This aim includes our self-project, our caring about others and the requirements of justice.
- This aim provides the context in which virtues relating to self-care, to interpersonal relationships and also to life in civil society can be felt as normative. Accordingly, virtue theory can embrace not only the commitments of character that constitute virtue, but also the requirements of justice that give form to those commitments.

Virtue is more basic than duty in that it requires virtue for us to acknowledge and debate what our duties are.

Although this discussion has given us plenty of hints as to what virtues will be important for us, it is time now, in Chapter 5, to spell out some of the virtues that are important in the contemporary world. We have spent a lot of time on moral theory in order to show that virtue ethics gives us a viable conception of what morality is and why virtues are normative for us, whether they be required by concern for others or by justice. We now need to spell out some of the virtues that we should seek to acquire.

five

Some important virtues

Introduction

In the course of the preceding chapters I have mentioned a number of virtues without giving a full exposition of what they were and why they should be considered virtues. It is now time to offer such an exposition and to list a number of virtues that I consider important for contemporary life.

We should first, however, note that the names of virtues are not like the names of items of furniture. All competent users of language would call a table a table (although there might be some pieces of furniture that leave us puzzled even though they are somewhat table-like). Tables are entities that exist in the world and that can, for all intents and purposes, be clearly distinguished from chairs, beds and cars. Such designations are relatively simple. Human behaviour, on the other hand, is complex. People act from a variety of motivations and their actions have a variety of effects, some foreseen and others not. It requires interpretation in order for us to make sense of all this and we use a variety of categories for this. If we see a boy scout helping a frail old lady across the street we would be inclined to interpret that phenomenon as an act of kindness but there would be plenty of scope for alternative interpretations. It might be that the boy scout wants to impress his peers, or it might be that he is motivated by a sense of duty rather than kindness. In describing it as an act of kindness we are not only interpreting the act but also attributing virtuous motivations to the agent and making assumptions about the contextual meaning of that agent's action. We use the names of virtues and vices as categories that we impose on the rich tapestry of human behaviour and character traits in order to interpret them and make judgements about them.

These categories are highly fluid. We could interpret the boy scout's action as an act of kindness, an act of caring, an act of compassion, or an act of generosity. Just how these distinctions are to be drawn is not clearcut. Not only is it difficult to know enough about the particular case to know which description applies, but it is difficult to differentiate those various categories conceptually. We cannot distinguish an act of kindness from an act of compassion as clearly as we can distinguish a table from a bed. In short, how we conceptually carve up the phenomena of virtuous human behaviour into specific virtue classifications is highly complex and probably culture relative. It is certainly relative to the resources of our language. The Greeks had several words for "love" (*eros*, *philia* and *agapē*) so that they were able to make relevant distinctions more readily than we can in English. That said, the English language is remarkably rich in virtue terms and permits us to make many subtle distinctions. Moreover, for every virtue category it seems possible to distinguish subcategories. Integrity, for example, can be expressed in honest actions or in authentic reflection about oneself.

We should accept the rich and complicated set of categories that our language has bequeathed to us. There are subtle differences between kindness, compassion, pity, charity, neighbourliness and caring, and it would serve no good purpose to obscure them by designating all those qualities with a single name. It would take the skills of literary writing to articulate these differences adequately, and some moral theorists have urged that philosophers should take more notice of literature and of the examples offered by literary characters in order to understand the virtues. It is a consequence of the particularism that is a feature of virtue ethics that one should not be too reliant on categories of a high level of generality. Given the specificity of the situations in which virtuous action and character are displayed, the nature of the virtue that is being displayed will also be highly specific. For all these reasons we are not likely ever to achieve a classification of virtues upon which everyone will agree. Nor does it seem necessary or conceptually useful to have such a definitive list.

Lists of virtues

Nevertheless, the history of ethics contains many lists of virtues. Table 3 is Aristotle's list as set out in the translation by J. A. K. Thomson of

Table 3 Aristotle's table of virtues

Sphere of action or feeling	Excess	Mean	Deficiency
Fear and confidence	Rashness	Courage	Cowardice
Pleasure and pain	Licentiousness	Temperance	Insensibility
Getting and spending (minor)	Prodigality	Liberality	Illiberality
Getting and spending (major)	Vulgarity	Magnificence	Pettiness
Honour and dishonour (major)	Vanity	Magnanimity	Pusillanimity
Honour and dishonour (minor)	Ambition	Proper ambition	Unambitiousness
Anger	Irascibility	Patience	Lack of spirit
Self-expression	Boastfulness	Truthfulness	Understatement
Conversation	Buffoonery	Wittiness	Boorishness
Social conduct	Obsequiousness, flattery	Friendliness	Cantankerousness
Shame	Shyness	Modesty	Shamelessness
Indignation	Envy	Righteous indignation	Malicious enjoyment

Book 2 of the *Nicomachean Ethics*. Note that the virtues are those traits listed in the column under the heading "Mean", and the states in the columns on either side are corresponding vices.

Not all of the virtues on this list would be readily recognized in contemporary Western societies. Magnificence, for example, is the quality of living grandly that ancient Greek society expected from its aristocrats and rich citizens, consisting of tasteful displays of wealth and supporting the city-state by funding public works and buying ships for commerce and war, for example. Today we expect the rich and powerful to be more understated in their generosity. Moreover, we tend to think that attributing a virtue to someone should not depend quite so much on that person's having abilities and opportunities that good fortune has given him rather than on his own efforts. Being rich is a prerequisite for being magnificent but it is not itself a basis for ethical praise.

Under the influence of the Christian tradition as well as of Aristotle, Aquinas listed four cardinal virtues – prudence, courage, justice and temperance – and three theological virtues – faith, hope and charity – and then subdivided each of these categories into a multitude of further virtue categories. In our own time, André Comte-Sponville lists and discusses politeness, fidelity, prudence, temperance, courage, justice, generosity, compassion, mercy, gratitude, humility, simplicity, tolerance, purity, gentleness, good faith, humour and love. In a discussion paper issued in 2004 by the Australian Victorian State Government, the following list of values was proposed as being appropriate for inculcation in schools (*The Age*, 29 October 2004):

- Tolerance and understanding – acknowledging other people's differences and being aware of others.
- Respect – treating others with consideration and regard.
- Responsibility – personal, social, civic and environmental.
- Social justice – the pursuit and protection of the common good. All are entitled to legal, social, and economic fair treatment.
- Excellence – seeking to accomplish something noteworthy, performing at one's best.
- Care – for self and others.
- Inclusion and trust – being included and including others, listening to others' thoughts and feelings.
- Honesty – being truthful and sincere.
- Freedom – enjoying the rights of citizenship, standing up for the rights of others.
- Being ethical – in accordance with generally agreed rules, and/or standards.

But perhaps the most comprehensive contemporary listing of virtues is that of Christopher Peterson and Martin E. P. Seligman in their psychology text *Character Strengths and Virtues: A Handbook and Classification*, which attempts to do for the personal qualities that make our lives go well what the *Diagnostic and Statistical Manual of Mental Disorders* does for the pathological conditions that vitiate our lives. They argue that the science of psychology has given more attention to our pathological conditions than to our healthy states of character and they set out to redress the balance. Their listing reads as follows:

1. **Wisdom and knowledge**: cognitive strengths that entail the acquisition and use of knowledge.
   - Creativity (originality, ingenuity): thinking of novel and productive ways to conceptualize and do things; includes artistic achievement but is not limited to it.
   - Curiosity (interest, novelty-seeking, openness to experience): taking an interest in ongoing experience for its own sake; finding subjects and topics fascinating; exploring and discovering.
   - Open-mindedness (judgement, critical thinking): thinking things through and examining them from all sides; *not* jumping to conclusions; being able to change one's mind in light of evidence; weighing all evidence fairly.
   - Love of learning: mastering new skills, topics and bodies of knowledge, whether on one's own or formally; obviously related to

the strength of curiosity but goes beyond it to describe the tendency to add *systematically* to what one knows.
- Perspective (wisdom): being able to provide wise counsel to others; having ways of looking at the world that make sense to oneself and to other people.
2. **Courage**: emotional strengths that involve the exercise of will to accomplish goals in the face of opposition, external or internal.
   - Bravery (valour): *not* shrinking from threat, challenge, difficulty or pain; speaking up for what is right even if there is opposition; acting on convictions even if unpopular; includes physical bravery but is not limited to it.
   - Persistence (perseverance, industriousness): finishing what one starts; persisting in a course of action in spite of obstacles; "getting it out the door"; taking pleasure in completing tasks.
   - Integrity (authenticity, honesty): speaking the truth but more broadly presenting oneself in a genuine way and acting in a sincere way; being without pretence; taking responsibility for one's feelings and actions
   - Vitality (zest, enthusiasm, vigour, energy): approaching life with excitement and energy; *not* doing things halfway or halfheartedly; living life as an adventure; feeling alive and activated.
3. **Humanity**: interpersonal strengths that involve tending and befriending others.
   - Love: valuing close relationships with others, in particular those in which sharing and caring are reciprocated; being close to people.
   - Kindness (generosity, nurturance, care, compassion, altruistic love, "niceness"): doing favours and good deeds for others; helping them; taking care of them.
   - Social intelligence (emotional intelligence, personal intelligence): being aware of the motives and feelings of other people and oneself; knowing what to do to fit into different social situations; knowing what makes other people tick.
4. **Justice**: civic strengths that underlie healthy community life.
   - Citizenship (social responsibility, loyalty, teamwork): working well as a member of a group or team; being loyal to the group; doing one's share.
   - Fairness: Treating all people the same according to notions of fairness and justice; *not* letting personal feelings bias decisions about others; giving everyone a fair chance.
   - Leadership: encouraging a group of which one is a member to get

things done and at the same time maintain good relation within the group; organizing group activities and seeing that they happen.

5. **Temperance**: strengths that protect against excess.
   - Forgiveness and mercy: forgiving those who have done wrong; accepting the shortcomings of others; giving people a second chance; *not* being vengeful.
   - Humility/modesty: letting one's accomplishments speak for themselves; *not* seeking the spotlight; *not* regarding oneself as more special than one is.
   - Prudence: being careful about one's choices; *not* taking undue risks; *not* saying or doing things that might later be regretted.
   - Self-regulation (self-control): regulating what one feels and does; being disciplined; controlling one's appetites and emotions.

6. **Transcendence**: strengths that forge connections to the larger universe and provide meaning.
   - Appreciation of beauty and excellence (awe, wonder, elevation): noticing and appreciating beauty, excellence and/or skilled performance in various domains of life, from nature to art to mathematics to science to everyday experience.
   - Gratitude: being aware and thankful for the good things that happen; taking time to express thanks.
   - Hope (optimism, future-mindedness, future orientation): expecting the best in the future and working to achieve it; believing that a good future is something that can be brought about.
   - Humour (playfulness): liking to laugh and tease; bringing smiles to other people; seeing the light side; making (not necessarily telling) jokes.
   - Spirituality (religiousness, faith, purpose): having coherent beliefs about the higher purpose and meaning of the universe; knowing where one fits within the larger scheme; having beliefs about the meaning of life that shape conduct and provide comfort.

This is an exhaustive and very helpful list and one that readers of Aristotle will find broadly familiar. Like Aristotle, Peterson and Seligman consider the traits of character that allow us to live full and fulfilling lives to be virtues. Moreover, many of the character traits that are to be thought of as virtues have benefits for others and for society.

Peterson and Seligman differentiate two levels of designation in this listing. The six numbered concepts are virtues broadly conceived. They are character traits that their empirical findings confirm are admired in all major world cultures. They are universal. But these virtues can be expressed in a variety of ways in a variety of contexts. The various admirable ways in which these virtues can be expressed are called "character strengths". So, for example, the virtue of justice can be expressed by displaying the character strengths of citizenship, fairness or leadership, depending on one's situation or social role. These character strengths may not be universal since social contexts and cultures differ, but Peterson and Seligman do refer to empirical studies that indicate that such character strengths are "ubiquitous" throughout the world. One advantage of their distinction between virtues and character strengths is that it introduces a structure into what would otherwise be a simple list. The character strengths are ordered under six broad headings that indicate what aspects of life they are relevant to.

Introducing some principle of order into lists of virtues is not new. Aristotle had also ordered his listings under the headings of virtues of character and intellectual virtues, and Aquinas speaks of cardinal virtues and theological virtues before he subdivides the members of each group into further categories. That there are numerous lists and several systems of classification in this way leads moral theorists to wonder whether there might not be a theoretical framework that would suggest a way of giving an intelligible structure to the classifications of the virtues.

One way in which moral theorists have attempted to bring order into the way in which virtues are classified and distinguished is to suggest that there are just one or two major virtues – call them "master virtues" – of which all the others are expressions. Peterson and Seligman do this with their group of six, but other theorists have spoken of a "unity of virtue" in which all the various virtues that they describe are claimed to be expressions of just one virtue. Aristotle said as much when he suggested that, in a mature person, the exercise of practical wisdom (*phronësis*) would lead to good actions. In a context of danger such well-judged actions might be described as courageous while in the context of distributing social goods they might be described as just. What is common, basic and generative of the virtue description in each case is that the agent has exercised good judgement concerning the situation and been sensitive to what is ethically important in it. In a similar way, the Christian tradition has urged that all the virtue and moral norms in accordance with which we should live can be summed up by, or generated from, the love of God. Provided we love God and receive his grace, all of our actions will be virtuous in various ways. All of these virtuous actions will express that single master virtue of charity, or love of God. Other theorists have claimed that we need only control our desires through the virtue of temperance in order to act well or that caring and benevolence sum up all the virtues. These are all attempts to bring order into the complex and variegated field of the virtues by seeing them as expressions of one or a few fundamental virtuous motivations.

I do not believe that this approach of positing a unity of virtues is of much help in the task of understanding what virtue is and of distinguishing one virtue from another. There is, however, an interesting psychological claim that is inherent in this approach: the claim that if a person is virtuous in one area of life then they are likely to be virtuous in other areas of life also. If a person is kind and caring towards those that are close to her, she is likely to be responsive to the needs of strangers as well. And this will give her a keen sense of fairness that might motivate her to act diligently and even courageously if the circumstances demand it, in order to pursue justice for all. Having some virtues very often leads to having others. To put the point negatively, it is difficult (although not impossible) to imagine a person who is selfish and unpleasant in some areas of life but who is kind and considerate in other areas of life. If these observations are correct (and they are empirical claims dependent on support by factual evidence), there would seem to be a psychological unity of the virtues. A virtuous person is likely to exercise a number of different virtues as different situations call for them. Moreover, as we shall see below, the exercise of one virtue very often also involves the exercise of others. But this does not imply that it is not useful to understand the individual virtue terms that we use and to distinguish them from other virtue terms.

I should also add that there can be pseudo-virtues or "imposter virtues". By this I mean that there can be character traits that are widely admired but that turn out not to be worthy of such admiration when placed under the scrutiny of Ricoeur's critical solicitude. Such critical thinking asks whether such traits really would be conducive to living life well with and for others in just institutions, and asks whether their exercise would be consistent with the principles of justice as discerned from an impartial and objective standpoint. One example might be competitiveness. In contemporary, free-market, capitalist societies the qualities that pertain to entrepreneurship are both useful and widely admired. These include prudence, willingness to take risks, leadership, decisiveness and competitiveness. Television shows such as *The Apprentice* show young would-be executives competing with one another in the successful display of these qualities. However, what is praised in such contexts as competitiveness very often involves insensitivity, short-term thinking, abrasiveness, selfishness and the willingness to sacrifice the interests of others for the sake of a paltry outcome. This raises the question as to whether competitiveness is a genuine virtue. That it is widely admired is not decisive on this point.

What I propose to do in the remainder of this chapter is to offer a description of a number of virtues that I consider important in contemporary Western societies. I shall structure the descriptions using a schema that explicates what it is to act from a virtue. I shall analyse three virtues below under the headings:

1. The field of the virtue – or what range of matters and sorts of things the virtue concerns itself with, or what sorts of situation call for the virtue in question (this is akin to the heading "Sphere of action or feeling" in Aristotle's list of virtues above);
2. The target of the virtue – or what virtuous actions of this kind seek to achieve in particular situations in that field;
3. The agent's feeling the appropriate emotion in the appropriate degree in relation to the situation;
4. The agent's knowledge of, and judgement about, the situation;
5. The agent's action in response to that judgement;
6. The beneficiaries of the virtue;
7. The moral significance of the virtue as seen from an objective and impartial standpoint;
8. The corresponding vices or failures of the virtue.

In order to illustrate how this schema works I shall begin by discussing a virtue that has already been mentioned in previous chapters: namely, courage. This has the further advantage of drawing together the various remarks that have been made about that virtue. Moreover, courage is a virtue that many classical and contemporary authors have found to be both important and paradigmatic of what a virtue is.

Courage

1. The field of the virtue

The field of this virtue is taken by Aristotle to be any situation that presents physical danger to the agent. Moreover, Aristotle specifies the field further in a way that anticipates heading 7. He specifies that courage can only be displayed in situations that involve positive moral value. As he puts it, the courageous man acts for the sake of what is noble.

It is only in such situations as the defence of the city against attackers, for example, that courage is displayed. If you face up to danger in the course of robbing a bank, then it is not courage you are displaying but some other quality, such as bravado. It would seem, then, that Aristotle is making it true by definition that courage is a morally good character trait.

It may be questioned whether this definition is in accord with contemporary usage. We admire bravery in sport even though that field of activity has little obvious moral significance. Many of us are apt to admire bank robbers as courageous when they act bravely and we express this admiration in much of our popular entertainment. We enjoy heist movies even if we expect the bad guys to get their just deserts. This latter expectation shows that we are equivocal in our admiration of courage when displayed by bandits, but the admiration still seems to be real. It is only when the perpetrators of wrongdoing are beyond the pale, morally speaking, that we refuse to admire even their bravado. The terrorists who attacked the World Trade Center in September 2001 were described as cowardly even though a more morally neutral judgement might have admitted that they faced death with great bravery. It seems that on this occasion at least, popular sentiment was in accord with Aristotle's way of describing the field in which courage can be displayed: that it is only displayed in the context of morally positive projects and situations.

Modern usage also differs from Aristotle when he confines courage to situations of physical danger. As Peterson and Seligman use the term, for example, you exercise courage in any situation in which there might be opposition to what you are doing in a way that would result in personal cost to you if you went ahead and did it. So, for example, if someone were considering exposing a corrupt practice in her workplace in a situation where she would almost certainly lose her job and attract the anger of her colleagues if she did so, it would take courage to do it. She is not facing the danger of death or physical injury, but there will be a cost to her. Courage would consist in overcoming the fear of this cost. We sometimes speak of "moral courage" in situations of this kind in order to distinguish them from situations requiring "physical courage", but the use of the term "courage" in either context shows that we consider that the same kind of character trait is involved in each case.

Modern usage also sanctions the use of the term "courage" in situations where a person is facing great hardship that she can do nothing about. For example, a patient dying of an incurable disease or someone whose spouse has died can be described as facing the situation with courage. Here the term means something more like "patience", "acceptance", "resilience" or "determination". It is not obvious that fear is the problem that is to be overcome here unless we consider the fear of death and of the ending of the joys of life. Rather, the person described as "courageous" is facing or having to accept a great loss and does so with equanimity. I consider this a metaphorical usage of the term "courage" and shall not consider it further here.

2. The target of the virtue of courage

The target of the virtue of courage is the doing of the deed that fear of injury or other bad consequences inhibits. It is important in this and in other cases of virtue to see that the target is not the exercise of the virtue as such or the training of oneself in it. You do not exercise courage in order to be courageous, to have others think of you as courageous, to be able to think of yourself as courageous or to train yourself to be courageous. These might all be effects that flow from the action, but they are not the target at which you aim when you act courageously. The target of a virtue is the specific expression of what Ricoeur had called our "ethical aim" as it is focused by the situation at hand. As we saw in Chapter 4, the aim of virtuous action is to live well, with and for others, in just institutions. This is a general aim and it becomes specific and concrete in a specific situation. This situation becomes the particular field of a particular virtue. In this way, when a city is being attacked by invaders the virtue that is called for from its soldiers is that of courage since the situation involves physical danger for them. In this situation, the target of this virtue is to defend the city against attack. In the situation where someone uncovers dodgy accounting practices at her place of work the target of the virtue is to expose the corruption. People do not do these things because they are the courageous things to do; they do them because, given their ethical aims, they judge that the situation calls upon them to act in that way.

If the target specific to the virtue of courage is that of overcoming the fear that would inhibit your doing what the situation calls for, you would not be acting courageously if you felt no fear of the bad consequences to you of doing it, whether because you are too stupid to see them or because your are "fearless". Doing the deed pure and simple is not the target. The target of the virtue is doing the deed in spite of the fear. Courage is a virtue of self-control. In this way, it is a virtue of the *way* in which we do things and is exercised in any of the many situations in life when fear of one kind or another has to be overcome. In this way courage is sometimes designated an "executive virtue", meaning that it can be shown in how one approaches a wide variety of projects that involve fear. Other executive virtues would include persistence, focus, enthusiasm and industriousness. These are all qualities that can be displayed in a variety of contexts, including some that might be of dubious moral worth. I shall return to this last point under heading 7.

3. The agent's feeling the appropriate emotion

The feelings that are appropriate in situations that call for courage will most obviously be various forms of fear. Aristotle highlights this when he says that courage is the mean between the extremes of fearlessness, which he calls rashness or foolhardiness, and cowardice, which is when our fear is so great as to prevent us from acting. According to Aristotle, the courageous person feels the appropriate amount of fear: an amount that reflects a sound appraisal of the dangers and costs inherent in the action that is being envisaged but is not so great as to inhibit that action. I would add that further feelings that would seem to be inherent in courage are determination and commitment. These are feelings that arise from the attitude that the agent has to the action that he envisages. It is because the Greek soldier-hero loves his city that he is determined to defend it against attack, and it is because the courageous worker is committed to the values of honest accounting that she decides to unmask the corruption she has detected. These feelings, arising from moral commitments and from our inherent ethical aim, motivate the courageous action and serve to overcome the fear that would inhibit it. Even in less morally significant contexts, it is the determination to win that motivates the courage of the sports hero. And in morally evil contexts such as that of 9/11, we can speak of the terrorists' fanaticism as the source of the feelings that allowed them to overcome their natural fear of death. In short, if courage is an executive virtue – a quality of *how* we do something – then the feelings that are appropriate to it will include not just the appropriate amount of fear, but also those feelings that motivate us towards overcoming the fear and performing the action in question.

4. The agent's knowledge of, and judgement about, the situation

In the case of courage, the agent's judgement about the situation will be similarly complex. Most obviously relevant will be his judgement about the dangers inherent in the situation. If he judges that there is no danger, then no courage will be called for. If he judges that the dangers are so great that the situation is hopeless, then it would not be courageous to act; it would be foolish. Then again, there might still be moral worth in making a hopeless gesture. The uprising of the Jews in the Warsaw Ghetto during the Second World War was hopeless, but as a gesture of defiance and an assertion of the right to exist as a people, it was a courageous act. Such examples show that the judgements relevant to the virtue of courage are not only judgements about danger and cost; they are also judgements about the values on behalf of which one acts. If one confronts great danger by climbing on to a high, slippery roof in order to retrieve a ball, even after a sound evaluation of that danger, one is exercising poor judgement because it is not worth taking such a risk for the sake of such an unimportant item as a ball. Courage being an executive virtue, the values on behalf of which it is exercised are as important as the virtue itself, and our judgements about the situation must reflect this.

5. The agent's action in response to judgement

The agent's action in response to the judgements that are relevant to courage will normally be to perform the action that fear inhibits. Unless that action is performed we do not describe the agent as courageous. The person who is stopped by fear from doing something that should be done is a coward. There will also be cases where the risk is not worth taking so that not performing the feared action is the appropriate thing to do, and in such cases "cowardly" is not the term we would use to describe the agent and the action; rather we might say they were sensible or prudent.

6. The beneficiaries of the virtue

The beneficiaries of a courageous action will be those, say, who are saved by the heroes who repel the invaders of the city: the citizens of the city that the soldier-heroes have defended. They will be the shareholders of the company whose books were being cooked. They will be the sports fans whose team has won as a result of the courageous play of the backline. They will be the Jews who are inspired to resistance by the self-sacrificing courage of their fellows in Warsaw. In short, whatever the value on behalf of which the courageous action was taken, those who endorse that value or benefit from it will be the beneficiaries of the virtue. But there is also a broader benefit for others. Courage as such is impressive and inspiring. It fills those of us who observe it with a new confidence in the qualities of humanity. It lifts our spirits. This is a benefit that is specific to the virtue itself and does not arise from the goals of the specific action that has been performed with courage. The citizens of the besieged city could be benefited in the same way if the enemy had simply given up and left; their city would be saved. But if they are saved by the courage of their soldiers in battle then a new level of value has been added to their history and traditions, and a new sense of the honour of that people has been added to their culture.

Moreover, the benefits of courage do not flow only to others. The agent benefits also. She achieves what she set out to do despite her fear and honours the values on behalf of which she saw it as necessary to act. She grows in confidence. She becomes more courageous in that she enhances her habitual character trait of being courageous. In more theoretical terms, she fulfils her ethical aim and achieves a form of *eudaimoniā*. In this way, and in common with many other virtues, she achieves self-fulfilment. At a more reflective level, she enhances her self-esteem. She feels good about herself. Moreover, we should not think of the benefits to the agent in purely individualistic terms. Aristotle's concept of the noble includes the idea of public honour and admiration. When he says that a person who acts courageously acts for the sake of the noble he means that that person will achieve an honoured status in the community as well as contributing to the honour and reputation of the community as such. Once again, these are not the targets of her virtue, but they are among its beneficial effects.

> Whereas courage is always respected from a psychological or sociological standpoint, it is only really *morally* estimable when at least partially in the service of others and more or less free of immediate self-interest.
> André Comte-Sponville, *A Short Treatise on the Great Virtues*, 47

7. The moral significance of the virtue

As we saw above, the moral significance of courage is ambiguous unless we agree with Aristotle that an agent is only courageous if she acts for a noble cause. In contrast to this attempt at making it morally good by definition, there are many who argue that, as an executive virtue, courage takes on the moral quality of the goal in pursuit of which it is exercised. The brave bank robber is showing courage even though his action is immoral. The vigorous footballer is showing courage even though his action is morally neutral. And the whistleblower is showing courage whether or not her action is morally worthy. Courage can be used for good or ill. That said, however, our intuitions seem to support the view that courage is a good quality in a human being. All other things being equal, and no matter what the nature of their activities, courageous people are more admirable than cowards. Courage is a positive human quality and adds to the goodness of life. Perhaps we can endorse this thought if we add that, like many good human qualities, courage is corruptible by evil intentions or can be used for evil purposes. That this is possible does not contradict the idea that, *prima facie*, it is an ethically good quality.

8. The corresponding vices or failures of the virtue

The most obvious corresponding vice or failure of the virtue of courage is cowardice. Aristotle would add rashness. But if we distinguish moral courage from physical courage, then we might also include as vices in this field obsequiousness, spinelessness and a too ready willingness to compromise. Indeed, one might even include laziness, lack of persistence and vacillation in this list. Hamlet's inability to take decisive action may be seen as lack of courage, for example, even though it was manifest as vacillation, lethargy, procrastination and self-doubt.

Now that I have tested and illustrated my eight-point schema with the relatively familiar virtue of courage, let us see how it will illuminate some further virtues.

Taking responsibility

This is not a virtue that appears on many lists, perhaps because there does not seem to be a single word to name it. I could also describe it as "being responsible" or as "willingness to take responsibility". The single word "responsibility" (used by the Victorian State Government in its list above) does not seem to capture the sense of it adequately. It is not the same as accepting responsibility in the sense of taking the blame or being accountable when something in which you are involved has gone wrong, although this may follow from it. I have in mind scenarios such as the following:

- In a relatively busy city street a woman is being mugged. She screams for help but nobody tries to help her.
- Although he recognizes that clearing his property of trees will increase problems of soil salinity, a farmer reasons that one more paddock will not make much difference to an already intractable problem.

- In a democratic nation where voting is not compulsory a great many people do not vote.
- The government needs to establish an institution to house people suffering from psychological illness. Several sites are proposed but local citizens object, saying "Not in my backyard" in so many words.
- A highly profitable corporation that is paying its third-world workers a pittance to manufacture its goods answers its critics by asserting that its only responsibility is to its shareholders.
- In the face of global warming, a government refuses to sign and implement the Kyoto agreement for limiting greenhouse gas emissions.

These are all examples of failures in the virtue that illustrate what the virtue of taking responsibility would entail. To take responsibility is to accept that it is up to me. I should not leave it to others to solve the problem. Moreover, the subject of this virtue could be the individual, as in the first three scenarios, a community or neighbourhood, a corporation or a nation-state, as in the further examples. How the last three cases translate into individual responsibilities depends on the structure of democratic decision-making in those communities, organizations or states. Someone has to stand up at the community meeting and convince the neighbourhood that it can accept and care for the mentally ill. Shareholders should hold the directors of the company to account at general meetings. And responsible citizens should vote for whatever party undertakes to ratify the Kyoto accords if it wins government.

1. The field of the virtue

The field of this virtue is the set of problems in the world with solutions to which I can contribute. This field is vast. There are countless problems in the world that I can help solve, ranging from putting out the rubbish at home to securing world peace globally. There is no doubt that my power to effect positive change varies as we move from the local to the global but in every case there is something I can do and some contribution, however small, that I can make. Being willing to help out in the domestic sphere and in the local community may have more obvious effects and benefits, but my willingness to become aware of wider social, national and international problems and to take whatever action is available to a citizen in my society is both a necessary and significant contribution to the common good.

Because the field of this virtue is so large, it may be questioned whether it is overly demanding. No one person, even if she holds a position of considerable power, can effect the changes that would seem to be necessary in relation to global problems. Is it realistic to expect people to take responsibility when their contributions may be ineffective? It is interesting to note that psychological studies of scenarios of the first kind above indicate that if one person goes to help, others will be more likely to render assistance also. At first people are hesitant because they hope that others will step in so that they can avoid becoming involved. It is when someone does step in that their hesitation is overcome. Solidarity helps people to take responsibility. Accordingly, this virtue will seem less demanding if there are opportunities for collective action and if there are institutions that channel and structure a collective taking of responsibility.

2. The target of the virtue

The target of the virtue of taking responsibility is the good outcome that one's contribution to the problem is seeking. So, in the first scenario, it is the safety of the woman who was being attacked; in the second case it is the alleviation of soil salinity problems; and so on. But in each case, too, there is some sacrifice that the agent is being asked to make. In the first case, the first persons to intervene are running some risk of physical injury if they attack the muggers (there are other courses of action one could take also). In the second case, the farmer has to bear the economic cost of giving up the use of the uncleared paddock. In the third case, the citizen has to go out and vote and also take enough interest in the relevant political issues and personalities to make that vote an intelligent one. Corporations might have to forego some profits in order to institute just hiring practices and so on. We should not think of the target of the virtue simply as the beneficial outcome, but also as the paying of the price that is necessary to achieve that outcome. Taking responsibility involves some necessary self-sacrifice.

3. The agent's feeling the appropriate emotion

The feelings that are appropriate in situations that call for the taking of responsibility include concern for the matter at issue. In the scenarios above, virtuous agents would feel concern for the woman being mugged, for the farmland environment, for the democratic politics of their society, for the mentally ill, for the exploited workers of the third world and for the global environment. These feelings are expressions of caring and sympathy for others and, as such, are also related to the virtue of generosity and the virtues of humanity that Peterson and Seligman have on their list. But feeling concern for these various matters is not enough. The key feeling is that of not leaving it to others. It is a feeling of personal involvement. It is a feeling of commitment. It is a feeling that it is up to me to do something. It is a willingness to make sacrifices in order to get involved.

Moreover, to further counter the charge that this virtue is too demanding, taking responsibility requires us to feel hope. The person who takes responsibility is optimistic. Even though she recognizes in many situations that the problem is huge and apparently intractable, she remains hopeful that her contribution and that of others who work with her on the problem can be effective. The virtue of hope, as described by Peterson and Seligman above, is closely bound up with the virtue of taking responsibility.

4. The agent's knowledge of, and judgement about, the situation

In the case of taking responsibility, the agent's judgement and knowledge will be as various as the situations in which responsibility is called for. If you are trying to rescue the woman being mugged, you will need to judge what is the most effective and safest way of doing so. The farmer needs to understand the effects of clearing his land and needs to study better methods of land management. The citizen needs to understand political processes so as to recognize that voting is essential in a democratic society. People in the neighbourhood need to understand the needs of the mentally ill and that their facilities need to be sited somewhere. Company directors need to be familiar with the principles of justice as well as with the best means for turning a profit. And nation-states need to understand that sovereignty does not excuse them from responsibility for the global effects of what they do within their borders. The knowledge that is required for these various judgements will range from immediate evaluations of need to highly complex and scientifically based risk assessments. But the most important judgement of all is that of seeing that nothing will happen if everyone leaves it to others.

5. The agent's reaction in response to judgement

The agent, the group, the institution or the society will not be deemed to be taking responsibility if it does not act. Clearly, the action that manifests the virtue of taking responsibility will be the action that tackles the relevant problem. The structure of such action is that of a response to a need or a value. Whether it is the need of the woman being attacked or the need to preserve the environment, the person or group that takes responsibility sees those needs and responds to them. This point brings us back to Levinas's theory. For him, you will recall, the call that emanates from the mystery and infinity of the other calls me to be responsible for him. My goodness and identity as an ethical being arise from my response to the call of the other. It is my responsiveness that defines me as a responsible being because it takes me out of the self-preoccupation that modern individualism encourages. And my responsiveness can be to other values as well as to other people. I may see something of beauty. I will be drawn to enjoy that beauty but I will also be called upon by it to preserve or protect it: in short, to take responsibility for it. Even though there will be many circumstances in which I have no socially sanctioned role in preserving or protecting it, I will be inclined to take responsibility in any situation in which that might be called for. When the rainforests, for example, are under threat, I will contribute to the movement that works for their preservation. When a building of heritage value is under threat, I will agitate to have it preserved. In this and many other ways, my taking of responsibility is an answer to the call that things of value send out to me to value and preserve them.

6. The beneficiaries of the virtue

The beneficiaries of a responsible action are also easy to identify in each of my scenarios above. They will be the mugging victim who is rescued, the environment, the workers in the third world and so on. But, once again, the benefits of taking responsibility do not flow only to others or to the things that are preserved. There are also personal benefits such as self-esteem and the growth in confidence that one can make a difference. These are benefits of self-affirmation, whether experienced at the individual level or at a group level. One fulfils one's ethical aim and thus one's individual and social being by taking responsibility. But what is interesting about this virtue is that it can be exercised by groupings such as neighbourhoods, corporations, institutions and societies as a whole. To the extent that such groupings accept responsibility and act responsibly their standing will be enhanced. The reputation of corporations that act as responsible global citizens increases their standing and hence, it is argued, their profitability. Nations that act responsibly are respected and enjoy increased standing in the world of international diplomacy. They enjoy "moral credit", which gives them influence on the world stage greater than they might attain through mere military might.

7. The moral significance of the virtue

Although it might be possible to take responsibility in the context of some nefarious project so that one's contribution would be morally disapproved of, the character trait in question is one that is always admirable in itself. No one likes a shirker. Taken in itself, to be prepared to contribute and to shoulder responsibility is a morally approved trait.

8. The corresponding vices or failures of the virtue

The corresponding vice or failure of the virtue of taking responsibility is the tendency to leave it to others, to bury your head in the sand or to pass the buck. The shirker says, "It's not my problem", "Let the government take care of it", "Why does it matter?", "They've got no right to ask it of me" and "It's too hard". Related to these stances are laziness, selfishness, insensitivity to others and to things of value, losing heart, hopelessness and indecisiveness.

Reverence

Reverence is a virtue that we can understand in the light of Aristotle's concept of contemplation: the activity of thinking about eternal things exercised by that aspect of our being that looks beyond the vicissitudes and contingencies of this worldly life in order to find meaning and understanding in a reality of higher value. There are links also with Aquinas's theological virtues, although reverence is not a virtue confined to those who adhere to religious faith. And Peterson and Seligman's virtue of transcendence is also relevant.

1. The field of the virtue

The field of the virtue of reverence is the world in so far as it contains things that are greater than we are. Indeed, it is the universe in all its grandeur. For those who have religious faith, it includes God. The world contains things of beauty and things that are sublime. It contains magnificent products of human ingenuity and creativity. It contains things that have existed for immense lengths of time. The world is now known to be a tiny speck in a universe of unimaginable size and complexity. Our own existence as intelligent beings is the product of incredibly complex and contingent processes spanning eons of time. There is a spiritual dimension to life that leads many to religious faith and inspires others with a sense of wonder and peace. All of these phenomena, which theorists gather together under the heading of "the noumenal", constitute the domain of the virtue of reverence. And we must not overlook Levinas's point that a person whom I encounter in face-to-face rapport is also infinite and mysterious in their presence before me. Accordingly, such a person too is an object of reverence and belongs within the field of the virtue. Moreover, it is possible to have reverence for ideas. The ideas of Truth, Justice and Beauty, for example, might have become objects of distrust in our cynical postmodernist age but we should not forget that they are the names of ideals of such moral and aesthetic importance as to have inspired many people to deeds of greatness. You do not have to be a moral realist and believe that these terms name actually existing normative realities to be inspired by what they represent. They are objects of reverence that we can make real by instantiating them in our lives. Lastly, we must not forget the importance of ritual in our lives. Rituals for which we should have reverence include family meals taken together, church services, civic and state ceremonies, marriage ceremonies, funerals, memorial services, prize-giving ceremonies and the like. These rituals demand reverence because a reductive and pragmatic form of instrumental rationality would dismiss them as irrelevant and unproductive.

2. The target of the virtue

The target of the virtue of reverence is to accord respect to those things that are wonderful and important. This may sound like a somewhat vague way of putting it, but this is because this virtue is primarily one of attitude. The reverent person seeks to contemplate the things that inspire awe in her, to be sensitive to the beauty and grandeur of things, to be respectful of others, to consider rituals important and to show deference to the gods. The virtue is evoked by the noumenal aspects of reality and the reverent person seeks to become attuned to the noumenal and to unite herself with it through silence and attention. The wonder and grandeur of the world and of what we take to lie beyond it is the object of the virtue. Our target is to protect, preserve and, in the case of God, worship that object. Beyond (or, perhaps, within) the humdrum rat race of ordinary life we sense a realm of beauty, spirituality and transcendence that, if we are seeking to live well with and for others in just institutions, we try to become more sensitive to.

> Reverence is the well-developed capacity to have feelings of awe, respect, and shame when these are the right feelings to have.
> Paul Woodruff, *Reverence: Renewing a Forgotten Virtue*, 8

3. The agent's feeling the appropriate emotion

The virtue of reverence involves feelings of awe, respect, gratitude, appreciation and even worship. When you are hiking and come across a sublime vista, the appropriate (and enjoyable) feelings to have are those of awe and appreciation. When you are in a concert hall and hear a wonderful and well-performed piece of music, the appropriate feelings to have are those of aesthetic appreciation and enjoyment of beauty. When you are in a church or temple, whether or not you are an adherent of the relevant religion, the appropriate feeling to have is that of devotion and surrender. Although the more frequent case would be one where religious believers express their faith in feelings of piety, you can be in a worshipful state of mind even if you do not subscribe to any theological or metaphysical beliefs. When you are at a ceremony the appropriate feeling to have is one of harmony with its movements and rhetoric. When you are in the presence of a friend or a loved one, the feelings of affection that you enjoy arise from a sheer delight in the very fact that that other person exists and that you are in their company. The fathomless mystery incarnated in their immediate presence before you evokes feelings of joy. And when you are talking to an older person who has experienced much in life or struggled against great hardships, feelings of respect and appreciation should colour your interaction with them.

But the quotation from Woodruff above also mentions shame. The obverse of feeling awe and respect for what is greater than me is feeling how small and insignificant I am. In the face of the immensity of the universe or the power of God, in the face of the beautiful and the profound, it is as if I am nothing. Once again, we see here the importance of humility. Although it is true that I am elevated and enriched by my contact with the transcendent, I am also humbled by it. The ancient Greeks used the term "shame" to express this. The opposite of this feeling or attitude was *hubris*: the feeling of being as grand and powerful as the gods. Many of the greatest stories of Greek literature recount how the mighty, the powerful and those who are filled with *hubris* are brought low and humbled by the gods or by fate. The greatest crime in the ancient Greek conception was to think oneself the equal of the gods or to think oneself able to harness the power of the gods for one's own purposes. It is better to feel shame and have a proper appreciation of one's vulnerability, mortality and finitude. This would be the attitude of the reverent person.

4. The agent's knowledge of, and judgement about, the situation

The core of the judgements that express reverence would be sensitivity. Because this virtue is focused on feelings and attitudes, the role of reason in these judgements is relatively small. The feelings of awe and wonder that the marvels of nature or of art should evoke in us have been silenced somewhat by the tendency of science to explain how such things work. Now that we know that the rainbow is produced by the refraction of light on vapour drops, can we still see it as magical? Science is said to have "disenchanted" the world. Pragmatic and instrumental thinking makes it more difficult for us to see the natural environment as inherently valuable rather than as an economic resource. The feelings of spirituality and piety that are evoked by the noumenal and that for many issue in religious faith are challenged by Enlightenment rationality, which finds it hard to believe in entities for which there is no evidence. The feelings of community solidarity that are evoked by ritual can be undermined by a sense that time is being wasted and more practical work needs to be done. The love and respect that we show to others can be undermined by theories that suggest that those reactions are so many strategies bred into us by the processes of natural selection. In short, the virtue of reverence depends upon our being somewhat less that rational, if being rational means being reductive, pragmatic and mechanistic. The form of judgement proper to reverence is that of responsiveness and sensitivity to the wondrous and the noumenal. It is intuitive and open-minded.

5. The agent's action in response to judgement

The actions that display reverence are those that preserve the things that reverence values. You would not harm that which you revere. If you are in awe of the beauties of nature or of the wondrous complexity and richness of biodiversity, you will want to preserve and protect them.

If you appreciate the cultural heritage represented by the arts, and by museums, churches, ancient buildings and historical places, you will support their preservation, upkeep and promotion in whatever way you can. If you are sensitive to the spiritual, you will adhere to your faith or respect the faith of others. If you are sensitive to the mystery and dignity of the other person, you will care for them and support them. If you understand the importance of rituals you will want to take part in them and not seek to rationalize them. This is a very broad and vague set of actions and one that cannot be delineated clearly. They are marked out as virtuous by the attitude of reverence that enlivens them.

6. The beneficiaries of the virtue

The beneficiaries of the virtue of reverence include those objects, ideas or persons that are preserved, cared for and protected by reverent people. But, once again, there is considerable benefit for the virtuous person as well. If Aristotle is right to suggest that there is an aspect of our being that seeks to contemplate eternal things, then it is a fulfilment of our being to be sensitive to the noumenal. It may involve the humble stance of knowing our place in the physical and social universe, but seeing ourselves as part of that wondrous natural world, or as a part of God's providential order, or as a beneficiary of the works of past generations, or as an object of the love of those persons whom we love, is an enhancement of our being. We may be puny in the context of the vast universe, but we have a place in it. We may be powerless in the face of the spiritual order, but we are also cosseted by it. We may have to suspend our independence and will to power, but the community and love that we gain through doing so enriches us immeasurably. In short, knowing our place gives us a place.

7. The moral significance of the virtue

Objective and impartial evaluation of the virtue of reverence does not yield clear results. It is not as easy to say why we morally approve of reverence as it is to say why we morally approve of honesty, for example. We do admire it, although perhaps we more often disparage its absence, but it is hard to say why. Perhaps this is an especially striking example of one needing to have the virtue in order to see why one should have it. If you are a disenchanted and instrumental rationalist you might regard the noumenal as so much hogwash. You might think that transcendent values are merely the product of ideologies, that art and heritage are simply resources to be exploited for the tourist industry, that religion is the opium of the masses, that the natural environment is a quarry to be mined for profit, that other people are human resources, that the aged are a healthcare problem, and that silence is nothing more than a respite from work. These views are not immoral as such. They involve no obvious injustice (although they might lead to exploitation). But they are terribly impoverished and a world based on them would be inhuman. Accordingly, the virtue of reverence should be morally approved.

8. The corresponding vices or failures of the virtue

The corresponding vices or failures of the virtue of reverence are ignorance, insensibility, philistinism, boorishness, crudeness, shallowness, lack of culture, economic rationalism, callousness, lack of appreciation, alienation, individualism, spiritual emptiness, *hubris* (including those forms of nationalism that claim that "God is on our side") and the lack of any sense of the relative importance of things.

Summary and conclusion

I began this chapter with some lists of virtues and asked whether there might be some way of ordering the virtues that are mentioned in them. Can they be grouped as to type or relevance? Perhaps they should be thought of as so many permutations of one single virtue or a few basic virtues. I suggested that there was not much to be gained by pursuing such questions and proceeded to discuss just three virtues – courage, taking responsibility and reverence – using a schema that displayed their important ethical features. I make no claim that these virtues are the only ones that could be thought to be important in these postmodern times. In Chapter 6 I shall discuss some virtues that are especially relevant to the kinds of practical issues that preoccupy applied ethicists. Again, my list of such virtues will not be exhaustive but it will serve to demonstrate that virtue ethics can have something useful to say about the practical issues that beset us today.

six

Virtues and applied ethics

Introduction

Applied ethics is an emerging field in contemporary philosophy that seeks to apply moral theory to practical problems as they arise in contemporary society. These problems include: issues of international politics, such as what moral limits apply to us in the context of war and terrorism; issues of bioethics arising from advances in medical science that permit us to control the very architecture of life; issues of business ethics, such as the relation between the profit motive and social and environmental responsibility; issues arising from conflicts between conscience and professional roles and responsibilities; issues arising from information technology, such as the limits of privacy and the control of information; and so on.

It will not be possible in this book to discuss all of these issues or any of the many others that might strike you as important, and nor will it be possible to discuss any one of them at great depth. However, in this chapter, I do want to illustrate how a virtue ethics approach might differ from the way the ethics of duty discusses practical issues and will do so with reference to the doctrine of the sanctity of life as this is used in bioethics. I will then discuss the way in which virtue ethics relates to professional roles, and complete the chapter by explicating a virtue relevant to many of the issues illustrated above: integrity.

The virtue of reverence and the sanctity of life

A great many debates in bioethics centre on the notion of the "sanctity of human life". Decisions made in relation to abortion, euthanasia, research using embryonic stem cells, human cloning, the harvesting of organs from the newly deceased and many other issues grouped together under the label "bioethics" are often made and debated with reference to the notion that human life is sacred. This idea expresses an absolute and universal prohibition against the taking of innocent human life and remains central to the way of thinking in ethics that stresses duty and obligation rather than virtue. It belongs to a discourse of morality conceived as a set of universal, objective, and absolute imperatives that have their grounding either in the commands of God (divine command theory), human nature (natural law theory) or reason (Kant's deontology). Moreover, the pursuit of satisfactory consequences (utilitarianism) often supports the doctrine of the sanctity of life by using "slippery slope" arguments, which suggest that if we take a life in an individually justified circumstance it may lead to a lessening of the respect for life in the community at large.

What is meant by the idea of the "sanctity of human life"? The word "sanctity" is a theological notion. The phrase "life is sacred" is also often used and this too, in using the word "sacred", evokes a theological idea. To be sacred or to have sanctity is to belong to the realm of God. However, the phrases "sanctity of life" or "life is sacred" are often used by people who are not religious believers. Such people will say that they are referring to "the right to life". They are asserting that every living human being has a right to have its life respected and protected and that every responsible agent has a duty to protect and even enhance the life of human beings. In this way, it will be suggested that the notion of "sanctity" belongs not to a theological discourse, but to a moral discourse that centres on such notions as "rights", "duties", "obligations" and "moral principles". Human beings will be said to have "moral rights" in such a discourse, and the notion of "person" will be invoked as the node to which such moral rights attach. (This is why it is thought to be important to decide when and if a foetus is a "person" when debating abortion.)

It is no accident that the phrase "sanctity of life" occurs in both the theological and the moral discourses. Historically speaking it can be argued that our moral discourse is a continuation of that theological discourse in secular form. It can be argued that the notion of obligation is a continuation of the idea of the command of God and that the notion of equal human rights is a continuation of the idea of all human beings being created in the image of God. The moral theorist's idea that in every situation there is one right thing to do – some one action that trumps all other available actions and renders them either morally neutral or wrong – is a hangover from theology in that it assumes a God-like view of that situation from which such a judgement can be made. It is in this way that the notion of a right to life can be seen as a continuation of the idea of the "sanctity of life". Our hesitation in relation to end-of-life and beginning-of-life decisions is an echo of the determination of earlier generations not to usurp the right of God to take and to give life. We must not play God by interfering in the processes of the creation, shaping and termination of life, since such a prerogative belongs in the theological realm. Our moral beliefs in relation to such matters, even when our thinking is secular, is coloured by the heritage of theology. Our moral discourse acquires its features of absoluteness, universality, objectivity and normativity from the theological discourse of which it is the heir. The notion of duty that Kant took as a given and that he then analysed as respect for the law, is a direct descendent of the idea of obedience to the law of God.

I have argued that the discourse of virtue ethics is to be distinguished from this moral discourse. By virtue of the features enumerated in Chapter 1, virtue ethics can be seen to belong not to the discourse of morality but to the discourse of personal fulfilment and of honourable social living. It relates to how we should live in the context of our communities and our traditions. The ideals of human excellence and of human flourishing in accordance with which we seek to live are a combination of existential striving for self-affirmation on the one hand, and a desire to live in harmony with others in just societies on the other. It is on the basis of this complex inclination towards self-fulfilment and towards caring about others and about justice that the notion of virtue develops. A virtue is a trait of character that allows us to fulfil our own best aspirations and to do so by responding in the most appropriate way available to us to the values and needs that are present in any practical situation that we might be in. Specifically, in situations where decisions have to be made about terminating a human life, one virtue that will be crucial is that of "reverence for life".

I explicated the virtue of reverence in Chapter 5 and now suggest that an appropriate object of reverence is life itself. Although most of us no longer think of life as a gift from God or as a mystery that is completely beyond the comprehension of modern science, we still hold it in awe and approach it with reverence. Even a rudimentary knowledge of biology and medicine will be enough to convince us that living things are amazingly complex. Their vulnerability, delicacy and preciousness inspire awe. They operate within incredibly fine parameters in order to survive and comprise interactive systems of almost unbelievable fertility. The very appearance of life on earth is a product of such low probability and so subject to chance as to tempt us to use the notion of "miracle" to describe it.

Life even has ethical qualities. It is described by Nietzsche as striving and appropriation with his concept of "will to power". And yet in the case of most animals, and also human beings, it involves nurture and care. It is red in tooth and claw and yet also creates the most rudimentary forms of bonding and of society. Albert Schweitzer sees in it a model of human virtue. For him it is both the object of our reverence and the central value around which we should model our own lives. As such it is an appropriate object of respect. Our attitude to life should include that of gratitude. Our very existence as conscious beings is due to the processes that have, over eons, resulted in the evolution of first conscious and then self-conscious life. We stand as the beneficiaries of the process that, although driven purely by chance and by the fecundity of nature itself, has resulted in the possibility of beings like us.

But we should remind ourselves that the noun "life" is an abstraction. It denotes a biological condition or category that, whether in the new phrase "reverence for life" or in the old phrase "the sanctity of life", is still too abstract to enter the discourse of virtue ethics. As an abstraction, the notion of "life" fits easily into the discourses of theology and morality. Because those discourses describe our duties in universal, objective and absolute terms, they cannot but use a generalist language full of abstractions. Although these terms will be important, especially as we debate law and public policy, they do not capture the moments of intimate engagement with what is precious and vulnerable in concrete situations when virtue is called for. Virtue ethics is particularist: it speaks of specific things. So instead of speaking of "life" we should be speaking of particular living things. This will issue in differing commitments to action as we approach animals, the biosphere or other human beings. And in the last of these it will issue in differing responses depending on the condition of the human being before us.

Reverent agents will be in awe of living things and see them as valuable in themselves. They will be things that are not to be used as mere instruments of our will, but valued for their own sakes. Such agents will show respect for living things, admire their biological natures, and handle them delicately. Should situations arise in which a life would have to be terminated, virtuous agents will feel regret at having to pay such a price for the sake of some other and more pressing good. Even if a goat, for example, is to be killed in order to feed a family, the way in which it is dispatched will express the reverence that is extended towards it. There will be rituals that ensure that suffering is reduced and that seek atonement for the unavoidable loss of life.

A virtuous person will respond to a newly born child with love and affection, but there will also be reverence for the sheer fact of its existence as a living being. Virtuous action will be caring, tender and reverent. Such action will typically be directed upon the preservation of life. It will seek to preserve what is seen as precious. It will seek to protect what is seen as vulnerable. But the kinds of considerations that might lead us to see an abortion or an act of euthanasia as the best available option in a tragic situation will also lead the reverent agent to make such decisions. It is not an expression of reverence for life to maintain in life a living thing whose life prospects are bleak beyond what could be humanly accepted. If a newly born infant is horribly ill-formed, or if a dying patient is in unrelievable pain, heroic and burdensome efforts at preserving life will not recommend themselves to a reverent agent. Nevertheless, it will be an expression of reverence in such a situation to regret the loss of life and feel regret at having to be its cause. The reverent person does not have the cold assurance of the duty ethicist who thinks that all that matters is having done the right thing. Being virtuous will lead her to be sensitive to the values and needs of everyone involved in particular situations, to take responsibility and to place the contextually appropriate value on life. Accordingly, the idea that life is sacred can be interpreted not as an absolute command or prohibition, but as an acknowledgement that life is an apt object of reverence. Life or death decisions should be influenced by such reverence, by caring and compassion for those involved, and by acknowledgement of the relevant social norms that apply to such decisions.

The virtue of reverence gives depth and quality to the ethical life. It recognizes the value and importance of what virtuous agents have to deal with in the world and does not allow the rationalist thinking of the ethics of duty to usurp the sensitive awareness of what is at issue in morally difficult situations. Reverence for life may not solve the many ethical dilemmas with which healthcare workers and policy-makers have to grapple by yielding general norms, but it will add depth and significance to their deliberations.

Professional roles

There is a context in which my account of virtues as practical orienta-
tions to the world takes on a further level of complexity. Following
Ricoeur, I have suggested that self-esteem is one of the values that is
at stake in acting virtuously in that there are benefits for the self in so
acting. Along with the target of the virtue and the benefits that flow to
others is the fulfilment of the self that comes through acting in accordance with the standards that one has set for oneself and in response to
the requirements of the situation. Virtuous agents attest to their values
when they act virtuously and thereby fulfil themselves and affirm themselves as virtuous. But, as Ricoeur acknowledged, the self is not a simple
subjective entity. It is in some part a social construct and an important
source of such a construction of the self is the role we occupy in society.
This is especially clear in the case of the professions. If you are a lawyer,
a teacher or a doctor, your sense of yourself and of what it would be
virtuous for you to do, will include your sense of what it is virtuous for
a lawyer, a teacher or a doctor to do. Let me illustrate this.

Suppose you are a doctor in a palliative care unit looking after
terminally ill patients. You are caring for an elderly patient dying of colon
cancer. She is in terrible pain and none of the standard doses of morphine
seem to offer her relief. She seems to have few family and those that do
visit her are greatly distressed at her suffering. They suggest to you that
her death might be hastened. You yourself feel deep compassion at the
apparently pointless suffering of this woman and sorrow at being able
to do so little to relieve her pain. Almost everything in you urges you to
administer a higher dosage of morphine although you know it would be
a fatal. If you were the woman's nearest kin, you would do it. But you say
to yourself that even though you see that it would be a virtuous thing to
do, *as a doctor* you cannot do it. You recall that the role of a doctor is to
preserve life and enhance health. The medical profession exists in order
to cure disease, repair injury and save lives. Accordingly, although you
see no moral objection to an act of euthanasia in this case, you feel that,
as a doctor, it would contradict your professional commitments and sense
of vocation if you were to perform it.

My purpose is not to endorse this decision or to condemn it. I
use it simply to illustrate the way in which a purely personal ethical
commitment and a professional commitment can be in conflict. At a
personal level, you think that euthanasia is justified in this situation,
but as a professional you think that you ought not to do it. In order
to understand how this dilemma might arise, it is helpful to recall

the notion of "community" as I developed it in Chapter 4 and also MacIntyre's concept of a "practice", which I described in Chapter 1. A profession is an excellent example of a practice in his sense. If the practice or profession of medicine pursues such goals as curing disease, repairing injuries and saving lives, the values the profession pursues include those of health and life, and one of its central virtues will be reverence for life. Accordingly, an individual who becomes a doctor will place a greater degree of importance on life than would any other person. She might consider that, although there are tragic circumstances in which a life might have to be taken, it is not part of the role of a doctor to take it. She might consider that it would not enhance the profession of medicine if that profession came to accept the role of not only curing disease, repairing injuries and saving lives, but also terminating life when that might be called for. Of course, this view will generate debate. After all, if people were to agree that euthanasia is sometimes justified then it might well be asked what profession should be involved in administering it.

But my purpose here is not to elaborate on this issue. It is simply to illustrate how the concept of a professional role introduces a new level of complexity into the question of what it is virtuous for an individual person to do. My sense of myself as a virtuous person is not just a function of my character and ethical convictions as shaped by my upbringing, but also of my professional role. All of the professions begin with a period of training and education in which the neophyte is given not just the knowledge that is relevant to the profession, whether it be medicine, the law or pedagogy, but also an understanding of, and a commitment to, the values inherent in that profession: values such as health, justice and knowledge. Such an education shapes the individual's ethical outlook and defines what it would be virtuous for a professional to do so long as that professional is occupying that professional role. A caring husband who happens to be a doctor and whose wife is painfully dying of cancer might assist her in achieving a more speedy and peaceful death. But he will do so as a husband. Were he to be asked to do such a thing for a patient as a doctor, he might be more hesitant. He might consider that such an act, even if permissible for a husband, is not permissible for a doctor. And this will be because doctoring as such inherently pursues the goals of curing disease, repairing injuries and saving lives. If the profession of medicine were to accept the task of assisting terminally ill people to die peacefully by hastening their deaths, then the profession as a whole would have to revise its goals. There is currently debate within the profession on this very question.

> Characterising the goal of a profession in terms of the substantive good it undertakes to serve helps us better understand appeals to the notion of professional integrity as a reason for refusing to carry out certain requests from patients or clients.
> Dean Cocking & Justin Oakley, *Virtue Ethics and Professional Roles*, 83

There is a further point that arises from these considerations. If professions have specific goals and values, then there will be virtues that are either specific to them or especially important within them. I have already mentioned reverence for life as a virtue especially relevant to healthcare professions. In relation to the profession of medicine, bioethicist Edmund Pellegrino has listed the following virtues as being especially important: fidelity to trust and promise, benevolence, effacement of self-interest, compassion and caring, intellectual honesty, justice and prudence. Oakley and Cocking give special importance to beneficence, compassion, truthfulness, trustworthiness, courage, medical humility (the preparedness to see when burdensome medical interventions would be futile) and justice. My own work in nursing ethics has focused most strongly on the virtue of caring as being central to that profession. In the profession of nursing, caring is not just a matter of doing the job of looking after the sick effectively. It is also a matter of having a warm, compassionate and benevolent attitude to one's patients. Many of these virtues would be relevant to other professions also. We would expect lawyers to be especially committed to justice for example, to respect confidentiality and to be trustworthy generally.

Indeed, the frequency of the mention of trustworthiness in relation to professionals is striking. Professionals have social power and prestige because they have knowledge that other people need in order to solve specific problems. It is because I do not know enough about medicine that I need to go to a doctor when I am sick. It is because I do not know enough about the law that I need a lawyer when I am being sued. Moreover, I entrust professionals with private and sensitive information about myself. As a result of being dependent upon them, people need to trust professionals and professionals need to be trustworthy.

These sorts of considerations do not apply only to professions. Given that they have goals and values built into them, there are virtues that are especially relevant to a range of practices. We would expect public administrators to be efficient and frugal as well as trustworthy and concerned for justice. We would expect plumbers to be conscientious and so on. Moreover, most of the virtues that appear on lists of this kind are virtues that we would admire in a wide variety of professional and occupational contexts.

They are not so much specific to practices as highlighted by them. They are traits of character that we admire in anyone in any situation but which we expect to see instantiated to a higher degree or more often in a specific practice to the extent that the goals of the practice call for them. We want everyone to be trustworthy, but we especially want our accountants to be so. We want everyone to revere life, but we especially want our doctors to do so. We want everyone to be caring, but we especially want our nurses, teachers and social workers to be so. We want everyone to love justice, but we especially want our lawyers to do so. Problems only arise when, as in my example of the doctor, personal convictions come into conflict with the virtues inherent in a professional role.

Take the example of a politician. The practice or profession of politics has as its goal the exercise of political power in order to secure the public good. The values that politics seeks are social order, security and justice. In a democratic society politicians represent the people in exercising their sovereignty on their behalf. They legislate on the basis of social consensus and administer the laws and social policies that have been agreed to through democratic processes. Given this role of mediating public consensus on social policy, the virtues that are especially relevant to the practice of politics include sensitivity to social consensus, toler-ance, truthfulness, trustworthiness and taking responsibility. But now suppose that a momentous political decision has to be made: for example, on whether to go to war. Suppose further that a political leader thinks that going to war is important for the valid political goals of the state but that the people are not inclined to support such a decision. Should that politician tell a lie about the enemy in order to secure the support of the people and of the international community? Given the virtue of truthfulness, telling a lie would not be virtuous. As a private individual an ethical politician would agree that, *prima facie,* telling a lie would be unethical and immoral in most contexts. However, for what he genuinely takes to be valid reasons of state, this politician decides that, *as a politi-cian*, it would be valid for him to tell a lie so that the nation could go to war with the support of the people. Here we have a further example of the split between personal conviction and the demands of a professional role that we illustrated with the doctor above, except that in this case it is the professional role that seems to license an action that personal ethical conviction would disapprove of. The politician may think that the stand-ards of truthfulness that apply to people in general do not apply to him as a politician because the onerous responsibilities of making decisions of state sometimes require him to tell lies for the sake of the greater good. This is a scenario that calls for the virtue of integrity.

Integrity

The word "integrity" comes from the same Latin root as the word "integration". It bespeaks the unity or wholeness of a person's virtues and ethical commitments. Accordingly, as a preliminary suggestion I could describe both the doctor and the politician in my examples above as lacking integrity because there is a lack of fit between their personal convictions and the way they think their professional roles require them to act. But this is a complex matter and one that I shall explore further below.

> The person who speaks the truth is honest, but we regard this character strength [integrity] in broader terms. It includes truthfulness but also taking responsibility for how one feels and what one does. It includes the genuine presentation of oneself to others (what we might term *authenticity* or *sincerity*), as well as the internal sense that one is a morally coherent being.
> Christopher Peterson & Martin E. P. Seligman,
> *Character Strengths and Virtues*, 205

In order to explore integrity more thoroughly, let us analyse integrity using the headings that I set out in Chapter 5.

1. The field of the virtue

We might be tempted to say that the field of the virtue of integrity is the self. Those theorists who speak of integrity as being the integration or unification of the various desires, values and commitments of the self, those who see it as faithfulness to the core commitments that constitute the identity of the self, and those who see it as the determination to keep oneself innocent of moral evil would certainly seem to suggest that this virtue concerns itself with the moral status of the self. Other theorists reject these views on the grounds that, for a person who is not at one with himself or who is not able to avoid compromising their most cherished values (such as our untruthful politician), integrity is still available. It would consist in his honest acknowledgement of that situation. But on all of these views, integrity would be primarily an existential virtue concerned with the self.

However, there is a social dimension to integrity as well. Persons of integrity are admired and praised by others because of their reliability, trustworthiness and exemplary uprightness. These are social qualities as well as personal ones. They are qualities that we look for in people in positions of trust and in people who have made commitments, given undertakings or entered into contracts. Accordingly, I would suggest that the field of the virtue of integrity includes the sphere of interpersonal undertakings such as promises, contracts, professional roles and public offices in which there can be temptations to gain advantages by exploiting the trust of others. It is the field in which the public places trust in officials, business leaders or other office bearers and in which such individuals are expected to be trustworthy. This field belongs to the public and interpersonal sphere and brings a person's private commitments into that sphere. Integrity is the virtue where a person's own expectations about herself and the public's expectations about her come together.

2. The target of the virtue

What is the target of integrity? What does acting with integrity seek to achieve in the field of personal ethical convictions and in that of public and interpersonal commitments? The view that has frequently been put forward is that it is the purity of one's conscience or the self-esteem that arises from having acted in accordance with one's commitments. But there is also the unity and wholeness of one's ethical commitments. The ethical commitments that one has should be exercised consistently in all aspects of one's life, including one's professional roles. Such consistency is thus a target of the virtue. Moreover, in view of its dual existential–social nature, I would suggest that a further target of integrity is honour. This will seem like an old-fashioned concept in this individualistic and cynical age, but it captures well the combination of self-esteem and public respect that a person of integrity deserves to receive. The person who stands by her word, fulfils her commitments and avoids all forms of corruption and duplicity is a person of honour. The description "acting with integrity" can be attributed to such a person. We honour those who act well and who we believe are acting consistently with their own convictions. Of course, honour will be a target of other virtues also, as Aristotle makes clear in his remarks about courage. What is distinctive about integrity is that it seeks honour in the field of public roles and interpersonal commitments. In this context honour arises from trustworthiness. This, in turn, connects with the existential concerns of the agent because trustworthiness arises from the adherence of the virtuous agent to her public and personal commitments.

3. The agent's feeling the appropriate emotion

The feelings that are appropriate to integrity will combine personal and individual feelings with feelings of responsibility arising from being the recipient of public trust. An official who is offered a bribe will feel abhorrence at the very idea of securing personal gain through the misuse of public office. She will feel a sense of pride in having been entrusted with public office and will feel that the offer of a bribe is an insult in so far as the person offering it assumes that she is corruptible. This may even give rise to anger. Virtuous persons who enter into contracts will likewise feel that their honour is at stake in fulfilling those contracts and will accordingly feel loath to break them. This sense of having a personal stake in fulfilling the trust that has been placed in them will fuel a feeling of determination to keep their word or honour their obligations.

However, such feelings will be more complicated for the politician in my example. We have envisaged him as genuinely considering that going to war is necessary for the public good. It is not the case that he is being tempted away from the standards of truthfulness by the prospect of personal gain. Indeed, he may consider that there are great political risks involved in the deception. He is torn between commitment to truthfulness and his responsibility for the affairs of state, which he thinks can only be served by going to war. His feelings will include love of country and concern for the good of the state. Perhaps it is his feeling for the vocation of politics that is crucial here, especially if it involves the conviction that a politician sometimes has to dirty his hands and put moral scruples to one side in order to get important things done.

4. The agent's knowledge of, and judgement about, the situation

As for the agent's knowledge in relation to the field of the virtue of integrity, this will depend on the practice in question. The world of business, where contracts are entered into, public administration and politics are all practices in MacIntyre's sense of the term. Accordingly, virtuous practitioners will be aware of, and articulate about, the values and virtues inherent in those practices. They will know how important trustworthiness and reliability are. The public official who has been offered a bribe will need to be able to clearly distinguish between benefits that are the legitimate reward of his employment and benefits that are improperly gained through the use of the power that comes with his position. To this end, many practices and professions have articulated ethical codes of conduct. The agent's understanding of the field of the virtue of integrity will include knowledge of these codes and some understanding of the norms and values on which they are based. These should provide a basis on which the make the appropriate judgements if particular individuals are not sufficiently sensitive to the important values of the profession.

However, the case of the politician is more difficult. Many consider that the vocation of politics requires its practitioners not to be too precious about the purity of their consciences and to be prepared to do whatever they consider will lead to the best social outcomes, no matter what moral principles or standards of virtue are compromised in doing so. If telling a lie is the only way to secure an outcome as important as national security then would it compromise one's integrity to do so? (Notice that this is a different question from that which asks whether it is right to do so. Deceiving the public may have been the right thing to do and yet it might have compromised one's integrity to have done it.) This is a difficult judgement. It involves asking whether one's honour is more important than the national interest. But then the honour of a politician is not just his own honour. The national interest might depend upon the honour of the national leader.

5. The agent's action in response to judgement

The action that the virtue of integrity calls for is to honour the trust that has been placed in you. Do the trustworthy thing. Do that which you are being relied upon to do. Honour and respect the trust that others have placed in you. Fulfil your own standards of virtue, and fulfil your own ethical commitments. Live up to the virtues inherent in your profession or practice. Do not break the contract. Do not accept the bribe. Do not deceive the people even if you consider that great good could come from it. In short, be honourable.

6. The beneficiaries of the virtue

Deciding who the beneficiaries of the virtue of integrity are is complex if we assume, as does Paul Ricoeur, that self-esteem, sociability with others and a just society are inherent aims of human existence. Those who stress the existential dimension of the virtue will say that its beneficiary is the agent. The self-esteem that integrity justifies is certainly such a benefit. If we are able to achieve consistency between our ethical convictions and the responsibilities of our roles we will feel unified and whole in our outlook on life. Moreover if we act in accordance with, and by reason of, our promises, public undertakings and the responsibilities of our roles, then those actions will be constitutive of our integrity and will win us honour in the community. In this way self-esteem and honour will be the prize of our actions even if they are not their goal.

However, in stressing the social dimension of the virtue, it will become clear that, all other things being equal, the person or persons to whom you have made commitments also benefit from your honouring them. They will obtain what they have been promised or what they had trusted you to provide. But it should not be thought that this is all the benefit that is involved. There is a difference between doing good for someone and doing that good when one has undertaken to do so. The utility of the benefit may be the same in either case, but the latter contains the extra good of being the fulfilment of an undertaking. Not only is this an extra benefit for the recipient because it will fulfil her sense of fairness and satisfy the expectations that your undertaking had produced, but it is also a benefit to the community as a whole. If members of the medical profession, for example, act with integrity in their professional dealings, if they honour the Hippocratic Oath, and if they do not defraud the government of medical funding, then that profession will enjoy good standing in the larger society and have fewer internal problems to deal with. This makes the profession a beneficiary of the virtue of integrity along with the individuals who benefit from doctors' beneficent actions and the individual doctors who display the virtue. It was in such a way as this that Aristotle considered that a city-state would be a beneficiary of the virtues of its citizens. Those who argue for the importance of trust as part of the "social capital" of contemporary society would also see that integrity benefits the community as a whole.

7. The moral significance of the virtue

From the point of view of critical and impartial reason the virtue of integrity has considerable moral significance. It has been a theme of this book that the discourse of duty ethics with its focus on obligation and obeying the law should be replaced with the discourse of virtue ethics with its focus on responsibility and responsiveness to values. This gives the concept of responsibility a new importance in moral thinking. What is the point of integrity in this context? Is it just the basis of self-esteem and existential self-assurance? Is it just the socially desirable appearance of reliability? It is more than both of these. On the existential side it is the basis of responsibility. Only if I can attest to myself as a consistent identity with consistent commitments over time can I accept responsibility, make promises and commit to ongoing projects. Only if I have integrity can I be responsible and take responsibility. On the social side it is the basis of the imputation of responsibility to me on the part of others. My integrity is not just projected into the world by me so as to inspire confidence in me on the part of others. It is accorded to me by those others to the extent that they judge that such confidence is justified. This is what it means for them to call me an honourable person. In this way I can be accepted into the community as a responsible contributor and participant. The judgement of others that I am a person acting with integrity is as important as my own reflective judgement that I am indeed acting from integrity. That I am a person of honour allows me to be a responsible member of the community because I will be entrusted with responsibility. My responsibility is not just an existential quality arising from my self-esteem; it is a social quality arising from my standing in the community.

This is why the politician cannot have it both ways. He cannot compromise his reputation and that of his nation for truthfulness and yet maintain his standing as a responsible person. His being an honourable person is not just a matter of his being satisfied in his own mind that he did the right thing; it is also a matter of his being seen to be honourable by society. It is not just a matter of his having fulfilled what he sees as a moral obligation to pursue the national interest; it is also a matter of his being acknowledged by the community as having acted honourably. If these two perceptions do not coalesce, he lacks integrity just as much as he would lack it if his professional actions did not accord with his own ethical convictions. He may think that, because he judged the lie to be necessary, he acted with integrity in telling it. But the virtue of integrity or of trustworthiness is a public matter. Integrity consists in the mutual alignment of private decisions with public judgements. No matter what justifying reasons he thought he had, the politician who lied to the electorate has compromised his integrity. If found out he will lose his honour. And this in turn will jeopardise his effectiveness as a politician and leader. Given his professional role, that his conscience is clear will not make up for this.

8. The corresponding vices or failures of the virtue

The vices or failures of the virtue that correspond to integrity would include all those traits that bring dishonour upon us and that bring us into disrepute. They will include deviousness, dishonesty, guile, untrustworthiness, being "on the take", bad faith and deceitfulness. Insincerity, pretentiousness and phoniness are also failures of the virtue. Of course, all disapproved traits of character bring shame and dishonour upon us and so we must try to understand what it is specifically about these vices that makes them the antithesis of integrity. What they seem to have in common is that they involve us in not presenting ourselves to the world (and possibly to ourselves) as we really are. They involve a mismatch between our personal convictions and our public declarations, avowals and actions. A bandit lacks honesty but a businessman who projects himself into the world as honest while engaging in fraud is not only dishonest but also lacks integrity. He projects a lie about himself into the public sphere. He asks people to trust him because of his position in society even as he abuses that trust. The official who accepts bribes is not only a cheat but also an abuser of public institutions. Over and above his greed and dishonesty he is a destroyer of the just society that it is our inherent ethical aim to establish in the world.

Summary and conclusion

This chapter has sought to apply the concepts of virtue ethics to applied ethics in the following examples:

- In bioethics, rather than seeking to apply absolutist concepts such as the sanctity of life, decision-makers should display reverence for life. While this does not unequivocally indicate what should be done, it does add to the description of what the decision needs to be sensitive to.
- Professional roles often carry with them their own conceptions of virtue, conceptions that may not apply in other walks of life. Conflict can therefore arise between the virtues specific to some professions, personal convictions and the ideals of virtue held in the wider community. The virtue of integrity seeks to overcome this conflict by stressing the need to act honourably in the public sphere as well as the need to be true to one's own values.

The discussions of this chapter and the previous chapters have demonstrated that virtue ethics is a theoretically sound and useful framework for understanding morality, discerning what we should do and be, advocating specific virtues relevant to current moral problems, and understanding the moral psychology of virtuous persons.

Questions for discussion and revision

one Distinguishing virtue ethics from the ethics of duty

1. Why do you think it is important to be virtuous? Can you think of a virtue that is not morally important?
2. What do you understand by the notion of "character"?
3. Why is it important for virtue ethics to say what it is to be a good human being? Is it possible for people to agree on what a good human being is?
4. What do you understand by "particularism"? Why is virtue ethics particularist?
5. Why is making a morally difficult decision a risk? Can this risk be overcome by appealing to moral principles?
6. How is Carol Gilligan's distinction between a "justice perspective" and a "caring perspective" relevant to the distinction between an ethics of duty and virtue ethics?
7. How would you distinguish "reasons externalism" from "reasons internalism"? Why does virtue ethics prefer the latter?
8. Explicate the concepts of "foundationalism" and "hermeneutics". What is the relevance of these concepts to our understanding of virtue ethics? Do you think it is impo rtant or even possible to seek the foundations for our moral norms?
9. What is the problem of relativism and why does it seem to be an acute problem for virtue ethics? How would you answer the charge of relativism if you were a virtue theorist?
10. Why does the ethics of duty tend to assume a dualistic moral psychology? What does it mean to say that virtue ethics is, by contrast, holistic?
11. What do you understand by the notion of a "social atom" and how is it relevant to the distinction between the ethics of duty and virtue ethics?
12. Why is the concept of "supererogatory actions" difficult for an ethics of duty but not for virtue ethics?

two Aristotle's ethics

1. What does Aristotle understand by "ethics"?
2. What is a "teleological explanation" and how does it apply to human beings?
3. In your own words describe an interesting or dramatic incident in your life. Then analyse that incident and the way you experienced it in terms of the four levels of existence that Aristotle has identified as parts of the soul.
4. What does Aristotle understand by "virtues of character"?
5. What would be the best way to develop someone's virtues of character?
6. Are all pleasures the same, ethically speaking, or are some finer than others? If so, why?
7. What, for Aristotle, is the role of reason in relation to pleasure?
8. What, for Aristotle, is prudence or practical wisdom (*phronësis*) and why is it so important to him?
9. How does Aristotle distinguish prudence from wisdom? Which is most important for our ethical lives?
10. What do you understand by "happiness"? Is there only one way of being happy or can happiness arise in different ways of life?
11. What is the role of the intellect in happiness?
12. Do you think bad people can be happy?

three A brief history of virtue from the Stoics to Levinas

1. What is Hume's view on the basis of knowledge and what are the implications of this view for moral theory?
2. Why does Hume think it is not possible to derive moral principles from reason alone? From what does Hume derive moral principles?
3. For Hume, what is the most important virtue to have in order to live morally?
4. Explain Nietzsche's concept of will to power in your own words.
5. Explicate Nietzsche's distinction between slave morality and master morality. What are the virtues that are promoted in each of these moral outlooks?
6. For Nietzsche, what is the most important virtue to have in order to live well?
7. Why are other people a problem for Sartre's conception of our existential mode of being?
8. Why does Levinas think that the Nietzchean–existential conception of human beings as self-affirming and free individuals is inadequate?
9. Why, for Levinas, is the existence of other people more primordial than my own existence?
10. How does Levinas argue that our most primordial mode of being is already ethical?
11. For Levinas, what is the most important virtue to have in order to live well?

12. Do you think it is possible or advisable to live this way in contemporary times?

four Reconciling virtue and justice

1. Why is it not adequate to account for our responsibilities towards others by extending Aristotle's conception of friendship to all others, or by expanding the circle of those we care about?
2. What is the methodological advantage of using a hermeneutic approach to question 1?
3. How does Ricoeur's theory combine what I called our "self-project" in Chapter 3 with our "caring-about-others"?
4. Why is it important for Ricoeur that the self not be a simple and single existential entity?
5. What is Ricoeur's concept of an "ethical aim" and what is its significance in his theory?
6. What virtues are suggested by this ethical aim as it is expressed in the discourse of ethics?
7. What virtues are suggested by this ethical aim as it is expressed in the discourse of morality?
8. What virtues are suggested by this ethical aim as it is expressed in the discourse of politics?
9. Why is tolerance important in Ricoeur's view?
10. What is the conception of the just person that emerges from Ricoeur's theory?

five Some important virtues

1. Study the lists of virtues given at the beginning of Chapter 5 and identify which one you think is the most important. Give reasons why you think it important and explain what the virtue consists in.
2. Are there any virtues or strengths of character that you consider important that are not listed?
3. Think of an experience in your life, whether it was an event that happened to you or to someone else, that illustrates the virtue of courage. Explain why it impressed you.
4. Think of an experience in your life, whether it was an event that happened to you or to someone else, that illustrates the virtue of taking responsibility. Explain why it impressed you.
5. Do you think you would be better off if you did not take responsibility when called on to do so?
6. Think of an experience in your life, whether it was an event that happened to you or to someone else, that illustrates the virtue of reverence. Explain why it impressed you.

7. Do you think it would be possible to live a full and rich human life without reverence? Give reasons for your answer.

six Virtues and applied ethics

1. Why do you think life should be an object of reverence?
2. Do you think that scientific research into the genetic bases of life is an offence against reverence? Give reasons for your answer.
3. How do you think a virtue ethics approach might consider the issue of euthanasia?
4. How do you think a virtue ethics approach might consider the issue of abortion?
5. Explain the link between specific virtues and professional roles.
6. Would it be virtuous for an accountant to gamble with a client's money if he won and made money for the client?
7. Should politicians suspend moral norms in order to secure the national interest? Think of some examples where this might have occurred and explain the issues.
8. Think of an experience in your life, whether it was an event that happened to you or to someone else, that illustrates the virtue of integrity. Explain why it impressed you.
9. Why is integrity an important virtue for holders of public office?
10. Why is integrity an important personal quality?

Further reading

one Distinguishing virtue ethics from the ethics of duty

For a good introductory summary of virtue ethics see Greg Pence, "Virtue Theory", in *A Companion to Ethics*, P. Singer (ed.), 249–58 (Oxford: Blackwell, 1991).

The essay that began the contemporary discussion of virtue ethics was G. E. M. Anscombe's "Modern Moral Philosophy", *Philosophy: The Journal of the Royal Institute of Philosophy* 33 (January 1958), 1–19. It is reproduced in Roger Crisp and Michael Slote (eds), *Virtue Ethics* (Oxford: Oxford University Press, 1997), and in Joram Graf Haber, *Doing and Being: Selected Readings in Moral Philosophy* (New York: Macmillan, 1993). The Crisp and Slote volume presents many of the seminal essays on virtue ethics, whereas the Haber book presents a range of moral issues in two sections: one on the ethics of duty and the other on virtue ethics. It also presents a number of the key essays discussing virtue ethics.

Another seminal essay is Michael Stocker's "The Schizophrenia of Modern Ethical Theories", *Journal of Philosophy* 73 (1976), 463–66, which also appears in both the Crisp and Slote anthology and the Haber volume, as well as in Robert B. Kruschwitz and Robert C. Roberts, *The Virtues: Contemporary Essays on Moral Character* (Belmont, CA: Wadsworth, 1987).

Books that challenge the hegemony of duty ethics include Bernard Williams, *Ethics and the Limits of Philosophy* (London: Fontana, 1985) and Alasdair MacIntyre, *After Virtue: A Study in Moral Theory* (London: Duckworth, 1981), which revived interest in Aristotle. Another author to point towards the value of the concept of virtue in the early days was Philippa Foot in *Virtues and Vices and Other Essays in Moral Philosophy*, 2nd edn (Oxford: Clarendon Press, 2002; first published 1978).

There have now appeared a number of further useful anthologies of articles, including Roger Crisp (ed.), *How Should One Live: Essays on the Virtues* (Oxford: Clarendon Press, 1996); Stephen Darwall (ed.), *Virtue Ethics* (Oxford: Blackwell, 2003); Ellen Frankel Paul, Fred D. Miller, Jr., and Jeffrey Paul (eds), *Virtue and Vice*

(Cambridge: Cambridge University Press, 1998); "Virtue and Vice", special issue of *Social Philosophy and Policy* **15**(1) (Winter 1998); and Daniel Statman (ed.), *Virtue Ethics: A Critical Reader* (Edinburgh: Edinburgh University Press, 1997), which also contains some of the seminal essays.

Authors of substantive books that have developed the concepts of virtue ethics in a variety of directions include Thomas Hurka, *Virtue, Vice, and Value* (Oxford: Oxford University Press, 2001). This book criticizes some aspects of virtue ethics but shows how a utilitarian can take virtue into account. Then there is Rosalind Hursthouse, *On Virtue Ethics* (Oxford: Oxford University Press, 1999), which is a thorough treatment from one of the major voices in the field. Christine McKinnon's, *Character, Virtue Theories, and the Vices* (Peterborough, Ontario: Broadview Press, 1999) also offers a thorough treatment. The work of Michael Slote is especially important. He has written *From Morality to Virtue* (Oxford: Oxford University Press, 1992), which is a non-Aristotelian text that argues that virtue is all about being admirable rather than being moral. In a later work, *Morals from Motives* (Oxford: Oxford University Press, 2001), Slote develops the thesis that virtue must involve such emotions as benevolence and sympathy.

Another notable author is Christine Swanton, whose *Virtue Ethics: A Pluralist View* (Oxford: Oxford University Press, 2003) gives us an interesting original thesis stressing virtue as responsiveness to values. Swanton makes use of some ideas from Nietzsche whereas Richard Taylor, in his *Virtue Ethics: An Introduction* (New York: Prometheus, 2002), presents a somewhat polemical book from a Nietzschean perspective, which argues that Christianity has suppressed the more noble virtues of the ancient Greeks.

A wide-ranging discussion of moral theory that is sympathetic to the virtue approach is Robert Audi, *Moral Knowledge and Ethical Character* (Oxford: Oxford University Press, 1997). The ideas about particularism in the text might be explored further by consulting Lawrence A. Blum, *Moral Perception and Particularity* (Cambridge: Cambridge University Press, 1994) and Brad Hooker and Margaret Little (eds), *Moral Particularism* (Oxford: Clarendon Press, 2000), which is a somewhat technical collection of essays on particularism. My notion of hermeneutics can be explored by consulting Charles Taylor, "Interpretation and the Sciences of Man", in his *Philosophy and the Human Sciences: Philosophical Papers, vol 2*, 15–57 (Cambridge: Cambridge University Press, 1985). The source of the example of money used in my argument about the social construction of morality was John Searle, *Mind, Language and Society: Philosophy in the Real World* (London: Weidenfeld & Nicolson, 1999), while my use of slavery as an example drew upon Adam Hochschild, *Bury the Chains: Prophets and Rebels in the Fight to Free an Empire's Slaves* (Boston, MA: Houghton Mifflin, 2005), which is an enthralling historical account of the English campaigns to end the African slave trade.

two Aristotle's ethics

The source text for this chapter (from which the quotations are taken) is Aristotle's *Nicomachean Ethics*, J. A. K. Thomson (trans.) (Harmondsworth: Penguin, 1953) (or any other edition). There are excerpts from this book in many of the anthologies mentioned in Chapter 1. There are numerous commentaries on Aristotle's *Ethics*. I have found the following useful: David Bostock, *Aristotle's Ethics* (Oxford: Oxford University Press, 2000); Sarah Broadie, *Ethics with Aristotle* (Oxford: Oxford University Press, 1991); John M. Cooper, *Reason and Human Good in Aristotle* (Cambridge, MA: Harvard University Press, 1975); W. F. R. Hardie, *Aristotle's Ethical Theory*, 2nd edn (Oxford: Clarendon Press, 1980); Gerard J. Hughes, *Aristotle on Ethics* (London: Routledge, 2001); Amélie O. Rorty (ed.), *Essays on Aristotle's Ethics* (Berkeley, CA: University of California Press, 1980); Nancy Sherman (ed.), *Aristotle's Ethics: Critical Essays* (New York: Rowman & Littlefield, 1999); J. O. Urmson, *Aristotle's Ethics* (Oxford: Blackwell, 1988); James J. Walsh & Henry L. Shapiro (eds), *Aristotle's Ethics: Issues and Interpretations* (Belmont, CA: Wadsworth, 1967).

In her "The Discernment of Perception: An Aristotelian Conception of Private and Public Rationality", in *Love's Knowledge: Essays on Philosophy and Literature*, 54–105 (Oxford: Oxford University Press, 1990), Martha Nussbaum explains how *phronēsis* involves sensitive awareness of a situation.

Books on Aristotelian themes include Elizabeth Telfer, *Happiness* (Basingstoke: Macmillan, 1980), which also includes discussions of Mill and Kant, and Jonathan Lear, *Happiness, Death, and the Remainder of Life* (Cambridge, MA: Harvard University Press, 2000). N. J. H. Dent's, *The Moral Psychology of the Virtues* (Cambridge: Cambridge University Press, 1984) is not a study of Aristotle as such, but is heavily influenced by him.

three A brief history of virtue from the Stoics to Levinas

A very useful survey of ethical theories can be found in Robert L. Arrington, *Western Ethics: An Historical Introduction* (Oxford: Blackwell, 1998). The writings of the Stoics come down to us mainly in fragments and commentaries but a good selection can be found in J. L. Saunders (ed.), *Greek and Roman Philosophy After Aristotle* (New York: Free Press, 1966). Michel Foucault, *The Care of the Self: The History of Sexuality, Volume 3*, R. Hurley (trans.) (New York: Random House, 1986) provides an interesting slant on the Stoics and other ancient philosophers, while Martha C. Nussbaum, *The Therapy of Desire: Theory and Practice in Hellenistic Ethics* (Princeton, NJ: Princeton University Press, 1994) is an excellent and very readable introduction to them. Nancy Sherman, *Making a Necessity of Virtue: Aristotle and Kant on Virtue* (Cambridge: Cambridge University Press, 1997) contains an interesting chapter showing how Kant was influenced by the Stoics.

The source texts for Hume are: David Hume, *A Treatise of Human Nature* parts II and III, any edition; and his *Enquiry Concerning the Principles of Morals*, any edition, but for a very useful overview, see Arrington's, *Western Ethics*. Relevant to Hume is Ruth E. Groenhout, *Connected Lives: Human Nature and an Ethics of Care* (Lanham, MD: Rowman & Littlefield, 2004), which gives us an interesting discussion of the emotions of caring and sympathy. Also relevant to Hume is Craig Taylor, *Sympathy: A Philosophical Analysis* (Basingstoke: Palgrave Macmillan, 2002). This is a complex but insightful work written from a Wittgensteinian perspective.

The most important of Nietzsche's texts for understanding his notions of virtue is *Beyond Good and Evil*, R. J. Hollingdale (trans.) (Harmondsworth: Penguin, 1973) (or any other edition). Nietzsche at his most flamboyant can be experienced by reading his *Ecce Homo, How One Becomes What One Is*, R. J. Hollingdale (trans.) (Harmondsworth: Penguin, 1979). A very accessible book of commentary is Arthur Danto, *Nietzsche as Philosopher* (New York: Macmillan, 1965). There are many good studies of Nietzsche around but this is still a classic for clarity. Jean-Paul Sartre's scenarios come from his *Being and Nothingness*, H. E. Barnes (trans.) (New York: Washington Square Press, 1966).

My presentation of Levinas is drawn largely from Emmanuel Levinas, *Totality and Infinity: An Essay on Exteriority*, A. Lingis (trans.) (Pittsburgh, PA: Duquesne University Press, 1969). This is a very dense book but a clear summary can be obtained from Colin Davis, *Levinas: An Introduction* (Cambridge: Polity, 1996).

four Reconciling virtue and justice

Philosophers who attempt to derive our social responsibilities from love and caring for individual others include: Nel Noddings, *Caring: A Feminine Approach to Ethics and Moral Education* (Los Angeles, CA: University of California Press, 1984); Peter Singer, *The Expanding Circle: Ethics and Sociobiology* (New York: Farrar, Straus & Giroux, 1981); and Michael Slote, *Morals from Motives* (Oxford: Oxford University Press, 2001).

For a collection of essays linking virtue with community, see Amitai Etzioni (ed.), *New Communitarian Thinking: Persons, Virtues, Institutions, and Communities* (Charlottesville, VA: University Press of Virginia, 1995). For a further communitarian analysis of virtue, see Alasdair MacIntyre, *Whose Justice? Which Rationality?* (London: Duckworth, 1988).

For a Christian perspective on love as a universal requirement, see Gene Outka, *Agapē: An Ethical Analysis* (New Haven, CT: Yale University Press, 1972). John Rawls's conception of justice is found in his *A Theory of Justice* (Oxford: Oxford University Press, 1971).

Paul Ricoeur develops his position in Paul Ricoeur, *Oneself as Another*, K. Blamey (trans.) (Chicago, IL: University of Chicago Press, 1992), chs 7, 8 and 9. The table used in the text to explicate Ricoeur is my own. For a thorough discussion of the nature of, and ethical requirements upon, political discourse, see William A. Galston, *Liberal Pluralism: The Implications of Value Pluralism for Political Theory and Practice* (Cambridge: Cambridge University Press, 2002).

five Some important virtues

For a truly comprehensive treatment (the book runs to 800 pages) of the virtues from a purely descriptive perspective and without any moralizing, see Christopher Peterson and Martin E. P. Seligman, *Character Strengths and Virtues: A Handbook and Classification* (Oxford: Oxford University Press, 2004).

For a thorough treatment of the cardinal virtues, including courage, and a discussion of how the ancient Greek conceptions of these virtues differ from the Christian conceptions, see John Casey, *Pagan Virtue: An Essay in Ethics* (Oxford: Clarendon Press, 1990). A further and excellent account of courage can be found in Douglas N. Walton, *Courage: A Philosophical Investigation* (Berkeley, CA: University of California Press, 1986).

André Comte-Sponville's *A Short Treatise on the Great Virtues: The Uses of Philosophy in Everyday Life*, C. Temerson (trans.) (London: Heinemann, 2001) is a popular and beautifully written account of many important virtues but it does not contain much theory to back it up.

For a discussion of the unity of virtues see John Hanafin and C. A. J. Coady (eds), *Unity, Separateness and Conflict in the Virtues* (Aldershot: Ashgate, 2005).

George W. Harris, in his *Dignity and Vulnerability: Strength and Quality of Character* (Berkeley, CA: University of California Press, 1997), argues that strength of character is not always the best way to conceive of virtue.

The virtue of reverence is discussed in Paul Woodruff, *Reverence: Renewing a Forgotten Virtue* (Oxford: Oxford University Press, 2001).

six Virtues and applied ethics

An interesting collection of essays applying the concept of caring to medicine and nursing is found in D. F. Cates, and P. Lauritzen (eds), *Medicine and the Ethics of Care: Moral Traditions and Moral Arguments* (Washington, DC: Georgetown University Press, 2001), whereas Edmund D. Pellegrino and David Thomasma, *The Virtues in Medical Practice* (Oxford: Oxford University Press, 1993) contains Pellegrino's list of virtues for doctors. For a further virtue ethics approach to problems in bioethics see Stan van Hooft, *Life, Death, and Subjectivity: Moral Sources in Bioethics* (Amsterdam: Rodopi, 2004). My essays on caring in health care are found in various journals but will soon be published together under the title *Caring About Health* (Aldershot: Ashgate, forthcoming).

A collection that includes essays on civic virtue and the virtues required of judges, and other political applications, is John W. Chapman and William A. Galston, *Virtue (Nomos XXXIV)* (New York: New York University Press, 1992).

Dean Cocking and Justin Oakley, *Virtue Ethics and Professional Roles* (Cambridge: Cambridge University Press, 2001) is the source of my ideas about professional roles and the virtues that belong to them, while a sustained treatment of abortion and other beginning-of-life ethical problems from a virtue ethics perspective can be found in Rosalind Hursthouse, *Beginning Lives* (Oxford: Blackwell, 1987).

For an Aristotelian account of integrity as a mean between fanaticism and wantonness, see Damian Cox, Marguerite La Caze and Michael P. Levine, *Integrity and the Fragile Self* (Aldershot: Ashgate, 2003). An account of integrity in terms of commitment to one's own core values is offered by Bernard Williams in "Integrity" in *Utilitarianism: For and Against*, J. J. C. Smart and Bernard Williams, 108–17 (Cambridge: Cambridge University Press, 1973).

For the importance of trust as part of the "social capital" of contemporary society, see Onora O'Neill, *A Question of Trust: The BBC Reith Lectures 2002* (Cambridge: Cambridge University Press, 2003).

For a utilitarian critique of the "Sanctity of Life" doctrine, see Peter Singer, *Rethinking Life and Death: The Collapse of our Traditional Ethics* (Melbourne: Text Publishing, 1994). Albert Schweitzer's arguments about ethics and reverence for life are in Chapter 21 of his *Civilization and Ethics*, C. T. Campion (trans.) (London: Allen & Unwin, 1923).

Index